The Older Adult Psychotherapy Treatment Planner

PRACTICE *PLANNERS*™ SERIES

Treatment *Planners*

The Complete Adult Psychotherapy Treatment Planner, Second Edition •
0471-31924-4 *book only* • 0471-31957-0 book + disk
The Child and Adolescent Psychotherapy Treatment Planner •
0471-15647-7
The Chemical Dependence Treatment Planner • 0471-23795-7 *book only*
• 0471-23794-9 *book + disk*
The Continuum of Care Treatment Planner • 0471-19568-5 *book only*
• 0471-19569-3 *book + disk*
The Couples Psychotherapy Treatment Planner • 0471-24711-1 *book only*
• 0471-24710-3 *book + disk*
The Employee Assistance Treatment Planner • 0471-24709-X *book only*
• 0471-24730-8 *book + disk*
The Pastoral Counseling Treatment Planner • 0471-25416-9 *book only*
• 0471-25417-7 *book + disk*
The Older Adult Psychotherapy Treatment Planner • 0471-29574-4
book only • 0471-29581-7 *book + disk*
The Behavioral Medicine Treatment Planner • 0471-31923-6 *book only*
• 0471-31926-0 *book + disk*

Homework *Planners*

Brief Therapy Homework Planner • 0471-24611-5
Brief Couples Therapy Homework Planner • 0471-29511-6
The Chemical Dependence Homework Planner • 0471-32452-3
The Brief Child Therapy Homework Planner • 0471-32366-7
The Brief Adolescent Therapy Homework Planner • 0471-34465-6

Documentation *Sourcebooks*

The Clinical Documentation Sourcebook • 0471-17934-5
The Forensic Documentation Sourcebook • 0471-25459-2
The Psychotherapy Documentation Primer • 0471-28990-6
The Chemical Dependence Treatment Documentation Sourcebook •
0471-31285-1
The Child Clinical Documentation Sourcebook • 0471-29111-0
The Couples and Family Clinical Documentation Sourcebook •
0471-25234-4
The Clinical Documentation Sourcebook, Second Edition •
0471-32692-5

The
Older Adult
Psychotherapy
Treatment Planner

Deborah W. Frazer

Arthur E. Jongsma, Jr.

JOHN WILEY & SONS, INC.

New York • Chichester • Weinheim • Brisbane • Singapore • Toronto

Library of Congress Cataloging-in-Publication Data

Frazer, Deborah W.
    The older adult psychotherapy treatment planner / Deborah W. Frazer
  and Arthur E. Jongsma, Jr.
      p.   cm. — (Practice planners series)
    Includes bibliographical references.
    ISBN: 978-0-471-29574-7
(paper/disk : alk. paper)
    1. Geriatric psychotherapy. 2. Psychotherapy for the aged.
3. Mental illness—Treatment—Planning.   I. Jongsma, Arthur E.,
1943–   . II. Title. III. Series: Practice planners.
    [DNLM: 1. Geriatric Psychiatry—organization & administration.
2. Patient Care Planning. 3. Mental Disorders—in old age.
4. Psychotherapy—in old age. WT 150 F848o 1999]
    RC451.4.A5F755 1999
    618.97'68914—dc21
    DNLM/DLC
    for Library of Congress   98-42397
                                           CIP

To my parents, with love, Ann Willets Lapham Frazer and Evan Wayne Frazer

—D.W.F.

To the Older Adults who give so much meaning to my life: Mom (Harmina), Dad (Arthur), and Mother-in-Law (Evelyn).

—A.E.J.

CONTENTS

PREFACE

Working with older adults is a privilege. As geriatric practitioners quickly acknowledge, the clinician is greatly enriched by the wisdom and perspective of the elderly. It is with great humility that we try to capture here some of the teachings of our older patients, friends, colleagues, students, and of course, our parents. The *Older Adult Psychotherapy Treatment Planner* attempts to blend this wisdom with the treatment planning system set forth in earlier *Planners* to help therapists provide thoughtful, ethical, compassionate, and effective treatment.

Perhaps the greatest challenge in writing this *Planner* is the heterogeneity of the older adult population. The problems, strengths, and therapeutic strategies for a 65-year-old, cognitively intact, physically healthy individual differ enormously from those for a 90-year-old, cognitively impaired, physically frail individual. In addition, site of service will often affect treatment strategy: an individual living at home with a family caregiver will require quite different treatment strategies than someone living in a nursing home or assisted living facility. We attempt to accommodate this variability for the different problems, but therapists will need to be especially sensitive to the unique situations, strengths, and challenges of each individual as they write their treatment plans.

The goals of this *Planner* remain the same as its predecessors: To stimulate thought, improve quality of care, and improve efficiency of documentation. In addition, because psychotherapy with older adults is a relatively new field, it is our hope that practitioners who have recently started geriatric practice will find this *Planner* useful as a learning tool. Many of the concepts were developed over years of training Postdoctoral Fellows in the specialties of geropsychology and geroneuropsychology. Newer practitioners are especially encouraged to follow up the references provided in the Bibliography, the Bibliotherapy suggestions, and continuing education opportunities in gerontology and geriatric practice.

—*Deborah W. Frazer, Ph.D.*
—*Arthur E. Jongsma, Jr., Ph.D.*

ACKNOWLEDGMENTS

I want to thank many individuals who were so important in the development of this book. First, of course, are our patients who taught us so much. Colleagues from Norristown State Hospital, Northeast Community Mental Health Center, and the Philadelphia Geriatric Center (PGC) provided many years of education to me, with special gratitude to Powell Lawton, Kathi O'Leary, Phyllis DeCuollo, David Funk, Kathy Starks, and PGC CEO Frank Podietz. Genesis ElderCare was very gracious in granting me a leave to work on the manuscript, with special thanks to President Rick Howard, Senior Vice President MaryAnn Timon, and Vice President Irene Fleshner.

My husband and son, Jack and Nicholas Malinowski, cooked, cleaned, shopped, washed, and played while Mom was at the computer—how can I thank you enough for giving me the time to tell this story?

—Deborah Willets Frazer, Ph.D.

These are the "Golden Years"—those years after retirement at age 65 when your body breaks down steadily; your sight and hearing fade gradually; and your mental agility, memory, and concentration wane. Getting old gracefully is truly a rare gift as it is so easy to complain about physical problems, become depressed over losses sustained, and resent the growing dependence on others. The chapters of this *Older Adult Planner* reflect the common problems struggled with by those who are living the Golden Years.

Both of my parents (89 years old) and my mother-in-law (75 years old) are in the middle of the Golden Years journey. I salute them and dedicate this book to them, as each has individual circumstances that he or she is facing: the loneliness of living without a spouse, many miles of separation from most supportive family members, and/or deteriorating physical health that requires total assisted living care from virtual strangers (angels of mercy in most cases).

My mother, on learning of my work on this book with Deb Frazer, insisted I include her words of advice for others who, like she, are living in a nursing home facility. She suggested a necessary coping skill for those who are completely dependent on others for personal care that includes toileting. "Do not ring the staff call bell too early, or you will not be ready when someone comes to bring the bed pan. But do not ring too late, either, because it may take someone a long time to get the bed pan to you. It's a learned, highly refined skill of perfect timing." Obviously, mother's mental activity is still very keen, even though her hearing, sight, and physical strength are significantly debilitated.

Although Dad can still beat me when it comes to throwing 10 horse-shoes for ringers (at least 4 for 10 for Dad and 0 for 10 for "Junior"), his arthritis, reduced vision, and limited mobility kept him from playing golf with me for the first time ever during my visit to Phoenix last Spring. It hurt me not to have him with me and his 75-year-old brother, Henry, on the fairway hacking, praising each other's good shots, and sympathizing with our more common poor shots.

My mother-in-law has her own recent health complications, but she is reluctant to "chase to the doctor about them just to take more pills." She can easily become depressed over the recent death of a sister-in-law, the debilitating stroke and dementia of her brother, and the even more recent death of her brother-in-law. Her close-knit family is being decimated by the ravages of old age. She lost her husband, my dear and memorable father-in-law, 10 years ago, and she has found it difficult at times to hold onto a sense of meaning in life, even though she is very meaningful to me.

So this book touches a cord of familiarity in me, as it probably does for most adults like myself in the "sandwich generation" of people in their fifties and sixties—concerned over children and grandchildren on the one hand and parents on the other. I have been blessed with supportive, interesting, and loving parents and in-laws. I now hope that they sense my caring for them is evident in this *Older Adult Psychotherapy Treatment Planner,* as it was written with them in mind and heart.

A word of much deserved appreciation for hours of tedious manuscript preparation goes to Jennifer Byrne, my excellent office assistant. She has made sense out of miles of my scribbles and arrows and scratch-throughs. My wife, Judy, has continually offered her encouragement and support to my writing endeavors. And finally, Kelly Franklin, editor at John Wiley & Sons, Inc., is the genius behind the *Practice Planner* concept and deserves much of the credit for the ongoing project.

—*Arthur E. Jongsma, Jr., Ph.D.*

INTRODUCTION

Since the early 1960s, formalized treatment planning has gradually become a vital aspect of the entire health care delivery system, whether it is treatment related to physical health, mental health, or substance abuse. What started in the medical sector in the 1960s, spread into the mental health sector in the 1970s as clinics, inpatient facilities, and agencies, began to seek accreditation from bodies such as the Joint Commission on Accreditation of Healthcare Organizations (JCAHO). For providers to achieve accreditation, they had to strengthen their documentation skills—particularly in terms of creating individualized, quantifiable treatment plans.

With the advent of managed care in the 1980s, treatment planning has taken on even more importance. Managed care systems insist that clinicians move rapidly from assessment of the problem to the formulation and implementation of the treatment plans. Once formulated, these treatment plans can help keep the provider and the patient focused on the purpose of treatment—and help catalyze progress toward change. Many Medicare recipients are now switching from traditional indemnity plans to managed care plans, and this trend is expected to accelerate in the future.

The 1990s have been a decade of unprecedented change in geriatric mental health. Outpatient psychotherapy (including services provided in nursing homes or assisted living facilities) was essentially unavailable to Medicare recipients before July 1, 1990. On that date, new Medicare regulations took effect that permitted psychiatrists, clinical psychologists, and social workers to bill Medicare for outpatient psychotherapy services without a stringent fiscal "cap" on the amount of service. Simultaneously, nursing homes have been undergoing regulatory reforms that require increasing attention to the psychological well-being of residents. Behavioral interventions are mandated before use of chemical or physical restraints; assessment and treatment of depression, anxiety, and other mental disorders are now required. In tandem with these regulatory changes, recent research has documented the high prevalence of mental

1

disorders in geriatric residential settings and its effect on morbidity and mortality. These research findings further substantiate the need for mental health services for the older adult. Slowly, as providers have been trained to treat the mental health needs of the elderly, psychotherapy has become available for older consumers.

By middecade, Medicare began to question whether clinicians were providing psychotherapy appropriately to elders. The provision of psychotherapy to nursing home residents and cognitively impaired individuals is especially controversial. In May 1996, the Office of the Inspector General of the Department of Health and Human Services issued a report entitled, "Mental Health Services in Nursing Facilities," charging that almost one-third of mental health services provided in nursing homes were not "medically necessary." Psychotherapy services to residents with a diagnosis of dementia were especially likely to be questioned. In addition, JCAHO and NCQA accreditation of nursing facilities and behavioral healthcare organizations are raising issues of outcome measurement, quality improvement, and integrated care planning.

In this context, it is critical that clinicians clearly document the "medical necessity," therapeutic strategy, and benefit of the mental health services. This includes a DSM-IV diagnosis; specific problems to be addressed; goals; and specific, individualized, and measurable objectives. Providers must be able to chart the patient's progress to demonstrate that the patient is benefiting from treatment. Within nursing facilities, treatment plans should be consistent with, and contribute to, overall care plans. Only through such effective, high-quality treatment plans can mental health providers establish the need and benefits of psychotherapy for the elderly, including the frail and cognitively impaired elderly. However, many mental health providers have little experience in treatment plan development, especially with older adults. Our purpose in writing this book is to clarify, simplify, and accelerate the treatment planning process.

TREATMENT PLAN UTILITY

Detailed written treatment plans can benefit not only the patient, therapist, treatment team, insurance community, and treatment agency or facility, but also the overall psychotherapy profession. The patient is served by a written plan because it stipulates the issues that are the focus of the treatment process. It is very easy for both the provider and the patient to lose sight of what the issues were that brought the patient into therapy. The treatment plan is a guide that structures the focus of the therapeutic contract. Because issues can change as therapy progresses, the treatment plan must be viewed as a dynamic document that can and must be updated to reflect any major change of problem, definition, goal, objective, or intervention.

Patients and therapists benefit from the treatment plan, which forces both to think about therapy outcomes. Behaviorally stated, measurable objectives clearly focus the treatment endeavor. Patients no longer have to wonder what therapy is trying to accomplish. Clear objectives also allow the patient to channel effort into specific changes that will lead to the long-term goal of problem resolution. Therapy is no longer a vague contract to just talk honestly and openly about emotions and cognitions until the patient feels better. Both the patient and the therapist are concentrating on specifically stated objectives using specific interventions.

Providers are aided by treatment plans because they are forced to think analytically and critically about therapeutic interventions that are best suited for objective attainment for the patient. Therapists were traditionally trained to "follow the patient," but now a formalized plan is the guide to the treatment process. The therapist must give advance attention to the technique, approach, assignment, or cathartic target that will form the basis for interventions.

Clinicians benefit from clear documentation of treatment because it provides a measure of added protection from possible patient or insurance company litigation. Malpractice suits are increasing in frequency and insurance premiums are soaring. Medicare investigations of fraudulent practice have targeted behavioral health companies and individuals. The first line of defense against allegations is a complete clinical record detailing the treatment process. This requires a written, individualized, formal treatment plan that is the guideline for the therapeutic process. Such a plan, coupled with problem-oriented progress notes, is a powerful defense against exaggerated or false claims. In addition, Medicare requires that mental health providers communicate with the older adult's primary care physician about treatment. Sharing a formal treatment plan can meet this requirement and form the basis for an integrated approach to care.

A well-crafted treatment plan that clearly stipulates presenting problems and intervention strategies facilitates the treatment process carried out by team members in inpatient, residential, partial hospital, or intensive outpatient settings. Good communication between team members about what approach is being implemented and who is responsible for which intervention is critical. Team meetings to discuss patient treatment used to be the only source of interaction between providers; often, therapeutic conclusions or assignments were not recorded. Now, a thorough treatment plan stipulates in writing the details of objectives and the varied interventions and who will implement them. In nursing home and assisted living settings, mental health providers are encouraged to attend care planning sessions, to share the psychotherapy plan, and to help the care team integrate the psychotherapy plan into the overall plan of care.

Every treatment agency or institution is constantly looking for ways to increase the quality and uniformity of the documentation in the clinical record. A standardized, written treatment plan with problem definitions, goals, objectives, and interventions in every patient's file enhances that uniformity of documentation. This uniformity eases the task of record reviewers inside and outside the agency. Outside reviewers, such as JCAHO, Medicare, and State Health Department surveyors, insist on documentation that clearly outlines assessment, treatment, progress, and discharge status.

The demand for accountability from third-party payers and health maintenance organizations (HMOs) is partially satisfied by a written treatment plan and complete progress notes. More and more managed care systems are demanding a structured therapeutic contract that has measurable objectives and explicit interventions. Clinicians cannot avoid this move toward being accountable to those outside the treatment process.

The psychotherapy profession stands to benefit from the use of more precise, measurable objectives to evaluate success in mental health treatment. Wherever possible, this volume is based on scientific evidence of the efficacy and effectiveness of the proposed interventions. With the advent of detailed treatment plans, outcome data can be more easily collected for interventions that are effective in achieving specific goals.

HOW TO DEVELOP A TREATMENT PLAN

The process of developing a treatment plan involves a logical series of steps that build on each other much like constructing a house. The foundation of any effective treatment plan is the data gathered in a thorough biopsychosocial assessment. As the patient presents himself/ herself for treatment, the clinician must sensitively listen to and understand what the patient struggles with in terms of family-of-origin issues, current stressors, emotional status, social network, physical health, coping skills, interpersonal conflicts, self-esteem, and so on. Assessment data may be gathered from a social history, physical exam, clinical interview, psychological testing, or contact with a patient's significant others. The integration of the data by the clinician or the multidisciplinary treatment team members is critical for understanding the patient, as is an awareness of the basis of the patient's struggle. We have identified six specific steps for developing an effective treatment plan based on the assessment data.

Step One: Problem Selection

Although the patient may discuss a variety of issues during the assessment, the clinician must ferret out the most significant problems on which to focus the treatment process. With older adults, especially those with cognitive impairment, the problem may be defined (and the referral made) by a family member, caregiver, or other treating professional. Usually a *primary* problem will surface, and *secondary* problems may also be evident. Some *other* problems may have to be set aside as not urgent enough to require treatment at this time. An effective treatment plan can only deal with a few selected problems or treatment will lose its direction. This *Planner* offers 27 problems from which to select those that most accurately represent your patient's presenting issues.

As the problems to be selected become clear to the clinician or the treatment team, it is important to include opinions from the patient as to his/her prioritization of issues for which help is being sought. A patient's motivation to participate in and cooperate with the treatment process depends, to some extent, on the degree to which treatment addresses his/her greatest needs.

Step Two: Problem Definition

Each individual patient presents with unique nuances as to how a problem behaviorally reveals itself in his/her life. Therefore, each problem that is selected for treatment focus requires a specific definition about how it is evidenced in the particular patient. The symptom pattern should be associated with diagnostic criteria and codes, such as those found in the *Diagnostic and Statistical Manual of Mental Disorders, Fourth Edition* (DSM-IV) or the *International Classification of Diseases.* The *Planner,* following the pattern established by DSM-IV, offers such behaviorally specific definition statements to choose from or to serve as a model for your own personally crafted statements. You will find several behavior symptoms or syndromes listed that may characterize 1 of the 27 presenting problems.

Step Three: Goal Development

The next step in treatment plan development is that of setting broad goals for the resolution of the target problem. These statements need not be crafted in measurable terms, but can be global, long-term goals that indicate a desired positive outcome to the treatment procedures.

The *Planner* suggests several possible goal statements for each problem, but one statement is all that is required in a treatment plan.

Step Four: Objective Construction

In contrast to long-term goals, objectives must be stated in behaviorally measurable language. It must be clear when the patient has achieved the established objectives; therefore, vague, subjective objectives are not acceptable. Review agencies (e.g., JCAHO and NCQA), HMOs, and managed care organizations insist that psychological treatment outcome be measurable. The objectives presented in this *Planner* are designed to meet this demand for accountability. Numerous alternatives are presented to allow construction of a variety of treatment plan possibilities for the same presenting problem. The clinician must exercise professional judgment as to which objectives are most appropriate for a given patient.

Each objective should be developed as a step toward attaining the broad treatment goal. In essence, objectives can be thought of as a series of steps that, when completed, will result in the achievement of the long-term goal. There should be at least two objectives for each problem, but the clinician may construct as many as are necessary for goal achievement. Target attainment dates should be listed for each objective. New objectives should be added to the plan as the individual's treatment progresses. When all the necessary objectives have been achieved, the patient should have resolved the target problem successfully.

Step Five: Intervention Creation

Interventions are the actions of the clinician designed to help the patient complete the objectives. There should be at least one intervention for every objective. If the patient does not accomplish the objective after the initial intervention, new interventions should be added to the plan.

Interventions should be selected on the basis of the patient's needs and the treatment provider's full therapeutic repertoire. This *Planner* contains interventions from a broad range of therapeutic approaches, including cognitive, dynamic, behavioral, pharmacologic, family-oriented, and solution-focused brief therapy. Wherever possible, interventions represent empirically validated therapies. Other interventions may be written by the provider to reflect his/her own training and experience. The addition of new problems, definitions, goals, objectives, and interventions to those found in the *Planner* is encouraged, because doing so adds to the database for future reference and use.

Some suggested interventions listed in the *Planner* refer to specific books that can be assigned to the patient for adjunctive bibliotherapy.

Appendix A contains a full bibliographic reference list of these materials. The books are arranged under each problem for which they are appropriate as assigned reading for patients and/or their families. When a book is used as part of an intervention plan, it should be reviewed with the patient or caregiver after it is read, enhancing the application of the content of the book to the specific patient's circumstances. For further information about self-help books, mental health professionals may wish to consult *The Authoritative Guide to Self-Help Books* (1994) by Santrock, Minnett, and Campbell (available from The Guilford Press, New York, NY).

The Bibliography has been added as a reference for therapists. It guides the reader to the original sources for empirically validated therapies, practice guidelines, and general works that are helpful to the geropsychological practitioner.

Assigning an intervention to a specific provider is most relevant if the patient is being treated by a team in an inpatient, residential, or intensive outpatient setting. Within these settings, personnel other than the primary clinician may be responsible for implementing a specific intervention. Review agencies require that the responsible provider's name be stipulated for every intervention.

Step Six: Diagnosis Determination

The determination of an appropriate diagnosis is based on an evaluation of the patient's complete clinical presentation. The clinician must compare the behavioral, cognitive, emotional, and interpersonal symptoms that the patient presents with the criteria for diagnosis of a mental illness condition as described in DSM-IV. The issue of differential diagnosis is admittedly a difficult one that research has shown to have rather low interrater reliability. Psychologists have also been trained to think more in terms of maladaptive behavior than disease labels. In spite of these factors, diagnosis is a reality that exists in the world of mental health care, and it is a necessity for third-party reimbursement. (However, recently, managed care agencies are more interested in behavioral indices that are exhibited by the patient than the actual diagnosis.) It is the clinician's thorough knowledge of DSM-IV criteria and a complete understanding of the patient assessment data that contribute to the most reliable, valid diagnosis. An accurate assessment of behavioral indicators will also contribute to more effective treatment planning.

HOW TO USE THIS PLANNER

Our experience has taught us that learning the skills of writing an effective treatment plan can be a tedious and difficult process for many clinicians. It is more stressful to try to develop this expertise when under the pressure of increased patient load and short time frames placed on clinicians today by managed care systems. The documentation demands can be overwhelming when we must move quickly from assessment to treatment plan to progress notes. In the process, we must be very specific about how and when objectives can be achieved, and how progress is exhibited in each patient. *The Older Adult Psychotherapy Treatment Planner* was developed as a tool to aid clinicians in writing a treatment plan in a rapid manner that is clear, specific, and highly individualized according to the following progression:

1. Choose one presenting problem (Step One) that you have identified through your assessment process. Locate the corresponding page number for that problem in the *Planner*'s table of contents.

2. Select two or three of the listed behavioral definitions (Step Two), and record them in the appropriate section on your treatment plan form. Feel free to add your own defining statement if you determine that your patient's behavioral manifestation of the identified problem is not listed. (Note that while our design for treatment planning is vertical, it will work equally well on plan forms formatted horizontally.)

3. Select a single, long-term goal (Step Three), and, again, write the selection, exactly as it is written in the *Planner* or in some appropriately modified form, in the corresponding area of your own form.

4. Review the listed objectives for this problem, and select the ones that you judge to be clinically indicated for your patient (Step Four). Remember, it is recommended that you select at least two objectives for each problem. Add a target date or the number of sessions allocated for the attainment of each objective.

5. Choose relevant interventions (Step Five). The *Planner* offers suggested interventions related to each objective in the parentheses following the objective statement. But do not limit yourself to those interventions. The entire list is eclectic and may offer options that are more tailored to your theoretical approach or preferred way of working with patients. Also, just as with definitions, goals, and objectives, there is space allowed for you to enter your own interventions into the *Planner.* This allows you to refer to these entries when you create a plan around this problem in the future. You will have to assign responsibility to a specific person for implementation of each intervention if the treatment is being carried out by a multidisciplinary team.

6. Several DSM-IV diagnoses, which are commonly associated with a patient who has this problem, are listed at the end of each chapter. These diagnoses are meant to be suggestions for clinical consideration. Select a diagnosis listed, or assign a more appropriate choice from the DSM-IV (Step Six).

Note: To accommodate those practitioners that tend to plan treatment in terms of diagnostic labels rather than presenting problems, Appendix C lists all of the DSM-IV diagnoses that have been presented in the various presenting problem chapters as suggestions for consideration. Each diagnosis is followed by the presenting problem that has been associated with that diagnosis. The provider may look up the presenting problems for a selected diagnosis to review definitions, goals, objectives, and interventions that may be appropriate for their patients with that diagnosis.

Congratulations! You should now have a complete, individualized treatment plan that is ready for immediate implementation and presentation to the patient. It should resemble the format of the sample plan presented on the facing page.

A FINAL NOTE

One important aspect of effective treatment planning is that each plan should be tailored to the individual patient's problems and needs. Treatment plans should not be mass-produced, even if patients have similar problems. The individual's strengths and weaknesses, unique stressors, social network, family circumstances, and symptom patterns *must* be considered in developing a treatment strategy. Drawing upon our own years of clinical experience, we have put together a variety of treatment choices. These statements can be combined in thousands of permutations to develop detailed treatment plans. Relying on their own good judgment, clinicians can easily select the statements that are appropriate for the individuals they are treating. In addition, we encourage readers to add their own definitions, goals, objectives, and interventions to the existing samples. It is our hope that *The Older Adult Psychotherapy Treatment Planner* will promote effective, creative treatment planning—a process that will ultimately benefit the patient, clinician, and mental health community.

SAMPLE TREATMENT PLAN

Problem: AGGRESSION

Definitions: Verbally abusive or threatening language directed at caregivers or other residents.

Easily becomes frustrated and hostile when unable to complete task.

Goals: Reduce intensity and frequency of aggressive behaviors and verbalizations, treating others with civility and respect.

Enjoy warm and caring relationships with personal caregivers, including staff and family.

Short-Term Objectives	Therapeutic Interventions
1. Cooperate with evaluation to identify medical, neuropsychological, and/or psychological causative factors of the verbal and/or physical aggression.	1. Refer to the physician for evaluation of medical conditions and medications (prescribed and OTC) that could be causing hostility and aggression.
	2. Conduct or refer for psychological evaluation to assess possible contributions of depression and/or anxiety to hostile and aggressive behavior.
	3. Conduct or refer for neuropsychological evaluation to determine if verbal and/or physical aggression is caused by the patient's inability to inhibit aggressive impulses due to a brain disorder; if so, work with the caregivers to control stimulus conditions.
2. Cooperate with an evaluation to identify the specific behavioral pattern of verbal and/or physical aggression.	1. Conduct a behavioral analysis through direct observation, patient and/or proxy report; detail frequency of episodes, time of day, location, precipitants and consequences, observed/reported mood and rationale, and response to suggestions for change.

(Continued)

3. Caregiver ensures the patient's emotional comfort.	1. Teach caregivers to avoid possible emotional triggers by doing the following: spend at least five minutes letting the patient talk it out, give backrubs, hold hands, sing or hum together, listen to quiet music together, encourage reminiscing, gently groom with hairbrushing or application of lotion, read a story together, take a walk together.
4. Engage in mutually satisfying, pleasurable activities on a daily basis with primary significant others who become targets of aggression (spouse, family members, caregivers, roommates).	1. Instruct the patient and the primary significant other to develop a list of mutually satisfying, pleasurable, feasible activities (e.g., taking a walk, eating a treat together, feeding birds, looking at photographs, going to an activity together, talking on the phone, grooming nails or hair).

ADL/IADL DEFICITS

BEHAVIORAL DEFINITIONS

1. Decline in ability to accomplish one or more basic Activities of Daily Living (ADLs) independently: bathing, dressing, grooming, eating, toileting, mobility/transferring.
2. Decline in ability to accomplish one or more Instrumental Activities of Daily Living (IADLs) independently: shopping, cooking, housekeeping, financial management, transportation, medication management.
3. Confusion or conflict among family, staff, and patient about cause for, or amount of, decline in ADL/IADLs.
4. Threat to patient's safety due to decline in ADL/IADLs, such as falls, malnutrition, adverse drug reactions, or infections.
5. Confusion or conflict among family, staff, and patient about level of supervision required in residence.
6. Conflict between expectations for and actual recovery of function after stroke, hip surgery, or other medical event.
7. Patient is unwilling or unable to use adaptive equipment to compensate for decreased function.

—. _____

_____

—. _____

_____

—. _____

_____

LONG-TERM GOALS

1. Identify cause(s) of decline in ADL/IADL functions and barrier(s) to recovery of function.

2. All involved persons (staff, family, physician, patient) reach consensus on cause(s) for disability, prognosis, and a care plan.
3. Increase supervision/assistance to enhance safety.
4. Resolve depression and anxiety that may be interfering with motivation to recover function.
5. Maximize capacity for independent functioning in ADL and IADL spheres.
6. Identify and implement compensatory strategies, such as adaptive equipment, that support independent functioning.
7. Adapt to current and expected level of function.

—. _____

_____

—. _____

_____

—. _____

_____

SHORT-TERM OBJECTIVES

1. Consent to participate in evaluation of functional decline if decisionally capable; surrogate consents if the patient is not decisionally capable. (1)

2. Patient, staff, and family describe decline in function in specific detail. (2, 3)

3. Cooperate with immediate measures to improve safety. (4, 5)

4. Cooperate with a medical evaluation. (6)

5. Cooperate with a psychological evaluation. (7)

6. Comply with a neuropsychological evaluation. (8)

7. Attend a physical therapy evaluation. (9)

THERAPEUTIC INTERVENTIONS

1. Obtain consent from the patient or surrogate to address problem of functional decline, including consent to discuss issues with others involved.

2. Explore with the patient, staff, and family their perspectives on the decline in the patient's function (e.g., sudden versus gradual; precipitated or accompanied by a specific illness, medication, or event; the patient's reaction to the decline).

3. Administer a structured instrument, such as the *Physical Self-Maintenance Scale* (Lawton and Brody, 1969) to objectively measure

8. Participate in an occupational therapy assessment. (10)

9. Cooperate with a speech/language evaluation. (11)

10. Accept and participate in a referral to a dietician. (12)

11. Cooperate with a recreational therapy assessment. (13)

12. Patient, family, and staff verbalize an understanding of cause(s) for decline in function. (14, 15)

13. Patient, family, and staff accept prognosis regarding recovery of function. (16, 17, 18)

14. Patient, family, and staff agree on care plan to improve function as much as possible. (19, 20, 21, 22)

15. Comply with recommendations to change medications, dosage, or scheduling to improve function. (6, 23)

16. Complete treatment for confounding or coexisting depression and anxiety. (24)

17. Complete treatment for rehabilitation of function. (25, 26)

18. Use adaptive equipment that can compensate for decreased function. (25, 26, 27)

19. Comply with rehabilitation recommendations for ongoing changes in lifestyle, and need for increased assis-

the patient's and others' reports of functional decline.

4. Evaluate the possibility of imminent danger to self, such as infections, malnutrition, falls, adverse drug reactions, and so forth.

5. Arrange for the patient's immediate protection through installation of safety devices (e.g., grab bars), addition of services (e.g., home health aide), or in severe cases, transfer to a safer environment.

6. Refer to a physician for evaluation of medical conditions (e.g., Parkinson's disease, stroke, arthritis) and medications (prescribed and OTC) that could be causing decline in function.

7. Conduct or refer for psychological evaluation to assess possible contributions of depression and/or anxiety to decline in functional ability.

8. Conduct or refer for neuropsychological evaluation to determine if functional decline is associated with cognitive decline.

9. Refer to physical therapist for an evaluation of mobility-related declines in function, such as balance, gait, endurance, ability to transfer, and range of motion.

10. Refer to occupational therapist for an evaluation of ADLs (e.g., bathing, grooming, and hygiene) and

tance with ADLs/IADLs. (28, 29)

20. Verbalize an acceptance of increased level of supervision or help necessary to assure safety or to compensate for decreased independent functioning. (29, 30)

21. Verbalize and resolve feelings surrounding increased dependency on caregivers. (30, 31, 32)

22. Identify activities that can be performed as substitutes for those activities that cannot be performed. (33, 34, 35)

23. Reminisce about former accomplishments and relationships that built self-esteem. (36)

___. _____
_____

___. _____
_____

___. _____
_____

IADLs (e.g., driving and cooking).

11. Refer to speech/language therapist for an evaluation of communication skills and swallowing function.

12. Refer to dietitian for an evaluation of suspected malnutrition.

13. Refer to recreation therapist for an evaluation of leisure activity function.

14. Discuss and integrate the results of the evaluations with the physician and rehabilitation professionals as appropriate.

15. Meet with the patient, family, staff, and other professionals as appropriate to give feedback about the nature, severity, scope, and causes of the functional decline.

16. Explain, or have rehabilitation professionals explain, the prognosis for recovery of function.

17. Encourage the patient, family, and staff to voice doubts and raise questions about causes/prognosis.

18. Explore with the patient and family their emotional reactions to evaluations, including denial, grief, feelings of hope or hopelessness, anger, and so forth.

19. Introduce concept of *excess disability* to the patient and family, explaining that often negative psychological or

environmental factors produce disability beyond that which is expected from physical or cognitive causes; by addressing the causes of excess disability, the patient's function can often improve.

20. Establish with the patient and family what functions might be improved through addressing psychological or environmental factors.

21. Establish with the patient, family, and rehabilitation professionals what functions might be improved through a formal rehabilitation program.

22. Propose and obtain agreement to a care plan that combines all relevant modalities, professionals, and family support.

23. Reinforce physician's recommendations regarding medications and other treatments that could positively impact ADL/IADL function.

24. Address the psychological components of excess disability. (See Depression and Anxiety chapters in this *Planner.*)

25. Motivate the patient to comply with rehabilitation treatment, providing an outlet for ventilation of frustration, but also providing encouragement and reinforcement for completed sessions.

26. Communicate regularly with rehabilitation professionals regarding the patient's goals, progress, and psychological status.

27. Provide follow-up for rehabilitation professional's recommendations regarding adaptive devices (e.g., walkers or electric carts, communication boards, adaptive utensils, dressing and grooming aids, specialized phones or computers, household safety devices, etc.).

28. Provide follow-up and monitoring for rehabilitation professional's recommendations regarding lifestyle changes (e.g., patterns of physical exercise, dietary habits, leisure activity schedule).

29. Provide follow-up and monitoring for rehabilitation professional's recommendations regarding increasing assistance with ADLs/IADLs by working with the family to decide on whether assistance is provided by family, friends, neighbors, or formal caregivers.

30. Explore feelings about increased dependency and feelings toward those providing assistance.

31. Provide an emotional outlet for the patient to discuss ambivalence toward, and conflicts with, caregivers.

32. Help the patient resolve conflicts with the caregivers

(see Interpersonal Conflicts chapter in this *Planner*) and adapt to greater dependency.

33. Have the patient, family, and caregivers identify all areas of preserved function.

34. Work with the patient, family, and caregivers to identify substitute activities for those that can no longer be performed, such as winding yarn in place of knitting.

35. Find alternative sources of self-esteem; for example, even if arthritic hands can't perform old tasks, they can be beautifully manicured.

36. Use reminiscence to identify and elevate the patient's lifelong sources of self-esteem. Teach caregiver to encourage reminiscence through verbal description of events and people, looking at photographs, playing music from earlier eras, and/or handling objects from earlier eras.

—. _____

_____

—. _____

_____

—. _____

_____

DIAGNOSTIC SUGGESTIONS

Axis I:

293.0	Delirium Due to (Axis III Disorder)
290.xx	Dementia of the Alzheimer's Type or Vascular Dementia
294.1	Dementia Due to (Head Trauma, Parkinson's Disease, Huntington's Disease, or Axis III Disorder)
290.10	Dementia Due to Pick's Disease or Creutzfeldt-Jakob Disease
294.8	Dementia NOS
291.2	Alcohol-Induced Persisting Dementia
294.9	Cognitive Disorder NOS
296.xx	Major Depressive Disorder
309.xx	Adjustment Disorder
293.89	Anxiety Disorder Due to (Axis III Disorder)
300.02	Generalized Anxiety Disorder
300.00	Anxiety Disorder NOS
316	Psychological Factors Affecting Medical Condition
995.2	Adverse Effects of Medication NOS
——	————————————
——	————————————

AGGRESSION/HOSTILITY

BEHAVIORAL DEFINITIONS

1. Several episodes of explosive, aggressive outbursts resulting in assaultive acts or destruction of property.
2. Verbally abusive or threatening language directed at caregivers or other residents.
3. Catastrophic reaction, including angry outbursts, thrashing, crying out, and extreme agitation when overwhelmed, frustrated, or embarrassed.
4. Significant tension and anger are evident in body posture and language (e.g., clenched fists or jaw, glaring looks, bulging eyes, hunched shoulders, tensed large muscles in legs and arms).
5. Blames others for misplacing objects or being unable to carry out tasks.
6. Easily becomes impatient and hostile while waiting.
7. Easily becomes frustrated and hostile when unable to complete task.
8. Refuses personal care (toileting, dressing, bathing, grooming), using hostile and threatening manner.
9. Planned hostile actions taken against other residents, such as running into another with wheelchair, pouring water on the floor to cause falls, or setting room temperature or television volume controls to annoy another.

__. _____
_____
_____
__. _____
_____
__. _____
_____

LONG-TERM GOALS

1. Reduce intensity and frequency of aggressive behaviors and verbalizations, treating others with civility and respect.
2. Identify early warning signs of explosive outbursts or catastrophic reaction.
3. Avoid situations that produce feelings of frustration, embarrassment, or impatience.
4. Substitute prosocial ways of expressing frustration, embarrassment, or impatience.
5. Resolve conflicts that underlie planned hostile actions toward others.
6. Complete personal care tasks without verbal or physical aggression.
7. Enjoy warm and caring relationships with personal caregivers, including staff and family.
8. Enjoy mutually satisfying and supportive relationships with other residents, especially roommate, in residential facility.

—. _____

_____

—. _____

_____

—. _____

_____

SHORT-TERM OBJECTIVES

1. Consent to participate in evaluation of physical and/or verbal aggression if decisionally capable; surrogate consents if the patient is not decisionally capable. (1)

2. Cooperate with necessary safety precautions to protect self and others from harm. (2)

3. Cooperate with evaluation to identify medical, neu-

THERAPEUTIC INTERVENTIONS

1. Obtain consent from the patient or surrogate to address problem of physical and/or verbal aggression, including consent to discuss issues with other involved parties (e.g., family, staff, and physician).

2. Evaluate severity of danger to self and others; take immediate safety precautions (including adding staff

ropsychological, and/or psychological causative factors of the verbal and/or physical aggression. (3, 4, 5, 6)

4. Complete treatment for confounding or coexisting depression, anxiety, medical conditions, and/or adverse drug reactions. (6)

5. Cooperate with an evaluation to identify the specific behavioral pattern of verbal and/or physical aggression. (7, 8)

6. Caregiver identifies and avoids possible antecedents to ("triggers" for) aggressive behavior. (8, 9, 12)

7. Caregiver ensures safety of the patient and self. (10, 11)

8. Caregiver ensures the patient's physical comfort. (13)

9. Caregiver ensures the patient's emotional comfort. (14)

10. Caregiver ensures suitability of environment for the patient. (15)

11. Caregiver presents tasks appropriately for the patient's level of frustration tolerance, comprehension, and physical ability. (16)

12. Caregiver communicates in a calm, pleasant manner, in spite of the patient's hostility. (17, 18)

13. Caregiver implements communication skills of calm, distinct, deliberate, simple, polite speech. (19)

or family coverage, removal from current environment, or medication) as needed.

3. Refer to the physician for evaluation of medical conditions and medications (prescribed and OTC) that could be causing hostility and aggression.

4. Conduct or refer for psychological evaluation to assess possible contributions of depression and/or anxiety to hostile and aggressive behavior.

5. Conduct or refer for neuropsychological evaluation to determine if verbal and/or physical aggression is caused by the patient's inability to inhibit aggressive impulses due to a brain disorder; if so, work with the caregivers to control stimulus conditions.

6. Discuss the results of the evaluations with the patient, family, physician, and staff as appropriate; develop and implement a plan to address treatable medical and psychological causes for the aggression.

7. Conduct a behavioral analysis through direct observation, patient, and/or proxy report; detail frequency of episodes, time of day, location, precipitants and consequences, observed/reported mood and rationale, and response to suggestions for change.

14. Verbalize interpersonal conflict issues with others (e.g., spouse, roommate, family members). (20)

15. Complete psychotherapeutic treatment for resolution of interpersonal conflict. (21)

16. Engage in mutually satisfying, pleasurable activities on a daily basis with primary significant others who become targets of aggression (spouse, family members, caregivers, roommates). (22, 23)

17. Verbalize or demonstrate positive feelings toward the caregiver or roommate. (24)

18. Verbalize or demonstrate feelings of security with, and appreciation for, caregiver. (25, 26, 27)

19. Caregiver feels supported and able to enjoy the benefits as well as endure the burdens of a caregiver role. (22, 23, 28, 29)

—. _____
   _____

—. _____
   _____

—. _____
   _____

8. Teach caregivers (family and/or staff) to keep behavioral records, establishing at least one week of baseline recording.

9. Analyze with caregivers the behavioral patterns, developing hypotheses about possible "triggers" of aggressive episodes.

10. Analyze with caregivers the early warning signs of verbally and/or physically aggressive incidents.

11. Teach caregivers to ensure safety of self and others: stay calm, call for help from only one other person, never fight back, don't pull away if grabbed (distract instead), be alert to trouble and get a safe distance away, try to get patient to a seated position, then leave area for cool-down period.

12. Teach caregivers to prevent aggressive episodes by avoiding trigger (or identified negative stimulus) conditions.

13. Teach caregivers to avoid possible physical triggers by doing the following: reposition the patient frequently; add or remove a sweater; take the patient to the toilet; offer water or a snack; check for constipation; give OTC pain medication; provide hearing aid, glasses, dentures.

14. Teach caregivers to avoid possible emotional triggers

by doing the following: spend at least five minutes letting the patient talk it out, give backrubs, hold hands, sing or hum together, listen to quiet music together, encourage reminiscing, gently groom with hairbrushing or application of lotion, read a story together, take a walk together.

15. Teach caregivers to avoid possible environmental triggers by accommodating the patient's preferences: adjust noise and stimulation level (TV, radio); lighting; temperature; social environment (being with more or fewer people); activity level (doing more or fewer activities); environment (going for a walk or a ride, allow the patient to feel fresh air, rain, or sun).

16. Teach caregivers to present tasks by introducing one step at a time; the caregiver does the task *with,* not *to,* the patient; distract the patient during personal care with something familiar to hold; praise often; stop if hostile, aggressive reaction is building and try again later.

17. Teach caregivers that emotions are highly contagious and communicated nonverbally—if the caregiver is hostile and angry, the patient is likely to become hostile and angry.

18. Use role-playing and behavioral rehearsal to teach caregivers: Never argue back!

19. Teach caregivers that it is important to communicate with a calm and cheerful manner; with respect; with guidance, not control; at eye level; from the front, not from the side or the back; by speaking slowly and clearly; by speaking with a loud, low voice if the patient is hearing-impaired; by always offering simple choices when possible.

20. Ask the patient to identify the issues in the interpersonal conflict: differing expectations, needs, goals, or values; differing or difficult personal styles, cultural differences, underlying anger.

21. Explain psychotherapeutic approach to resolution of an interpersonal conflict, and obtain a commitment from the patient and the other party to participate in resolution process. (See Interpersonal Conflict chapter in this *Planner.*)

22. Instruct the patient and the primary significant other to develop a list of mutually satisfying, pleasurable, feasible activities (e.g., taking a walk, eating a treat together, feeding birds, looking at photographs, going to an activity together, talking

on the phone, grooming
nails or hair).

23. Help the patient and significant other to engage in one small pleasurable activity per day together.

24. Work with the individual who is the target of aggression to identify positive stimulus to consistently present at the beginning of interaction with patient (minicandy; newspaper or magazine; furry puppet).

25. Advise facility to use primary assignment staffing pattern (i.e., the same staff attend to patient every day) so that personal relationships can develop between staff caregivers and patient.

26. Teach staff caregivers to learn about patient's history by encouraging reminiscing and talking with the family.

27. Teach staff and family caregivers to ask questions that an individual with dementia can usually answer: multiple-choice or yes/no, tapping remote versus recent memory, asking about emotionally meaningful memories (e.g., name of a childhood pet).

28. Encourage caregivers to care for themselves: seek out social support; use respite care; don't take hostility personally ("it's the disease"); manage stress with diet, exercise, diver-

sions, relaxation, and caregiver support groups.

29. Recommend to the facility
that staff caregivers should
be provided with a support
group.

__. _____

_____

__. _____

_____

__. _____

_____

DIAGNOSTIC SUGGESTIONS

Axis I:	293.0	Delirium Due to (Axis III Disorder)
	290.xx	Dementia of the Alzheimer's Type or Vascular Dementia, with Behavioral Disturbance
	294.1	Dementia Due to (Head Trauma, Parkinson's Disease, Huntington's Disease, or Axis III Disorder)
	290.10	Dementia Due to Pick's Disease or Creutzfeldt-Jakob Disease
	294.8	Dementia NOS
	291.2	Alcohol-Induced Persisting Dementia
	294.9	Cognitive Disorder NOS
	310.1	Personality Change Due to (Axis III Disorder), Aggressive Type
	296.xx	Major Depressive Disorder
	309.xx	Adjustment Disorder
	293.89	Anxiety Disorder Due to (Axis III Disorder)
	300.02	Generalized Anxiety Disorder
	300.00	Anxiety Disorder NOS
	316	Psychological Factors Affecting Medical Condition
	995.2	Adverse Effects of Medication NOS
	_____	_____
	_____	_____

ANXIETY

BEHAVIORAL DEFINITIONS

1. Excessive fear and worry about life and health circumstances.
2. Inability to control worries about health, family members, social relationships, volunteer or job responsibilities.
3. Fear, worry, and other symptoms cause social withdrawal and sleeplessness.
4. Fear of doing or saying something embarrassing in a social situation, especially due to actual or feared memory or hearing impairment.
5. Fear, worry, and other symptoms significantly interfere with daily functioning at home, work, volunteering role, with family, or in social situations.
6. Symptoms of autonomic hyperactivity, such as palpitations, chest pain, shortness of breath, sweaty palms, dry mouth, trouble swallowing, nausea, or diarrhea.
7. Symptoms of motor tension, such as restlessness, fatigue, trembling, or shakiness.
8. Symptoms of altered cognition, such as difficulty concentrating, mind going blank, feelings of unreality, or feelings of being detached from oneself.
9. Symptoms of hypervigilance, such as feeling constantly on edge, sleep disturbance, and irritability.
10. Development of a dependence on substances to control anxiety symptoms.

—. _____
   _____
—. _____
   _____
—. _____
   _____

LONG-TERM GOALS

1. Significantly reduce the overall frequency and intensity of the anxiety symptoms so that the patient can improve daily functioning.
2. Decrease worry and fearful thoughts and increase optimistic, problem-solving thoughts.
3. End substance use as a means of escaping anxiety and increase constructive coping behaviors.
4. Decrease fear of social embarrassment and learn adaptive social skills.
5. Learn stress management skills to prevent anxiety response.
6. Learn problem-solving skills to resolve anxiety-producing problems.
7. Manage environmental stressors in a way to reduce psychological pressure.
8. Accept help as necessary from formal and informal support systems to reduce stress.

—. _____
   _____
—. _____
   _____
—. _____
   _____

SHORT-TERM OBJECTIVES

1. Identify the specific anxiety symptoms that are personally most disturbing or most contribute to impaired functioning. (1, 2)
2. Verbalize an understanding of the general physical and cognitive manifestations of and causes for anxiety. (3, 4, 5)
3. Keep a daily journal of anxiety symptoms for one week to establish frequency,

THERAPEUTIC INTERVENTIONS

1. Assign the patient to verbalize or list all specific anxiety symptoms in detail and to rank-order the symptoms on the basis of how disturbing they are.
2. Help the patient to identify whether and/or how each symptom interferes with daily functioning and/or relationships.
3. Teach the patient the anxiety symptom clusters: auto-

intensity, time of day, and duration of symptoms. (6)

4. Compile a list of all prescribed and OTC medications, dosage, and time of day they are taken. (7)

5. Compile a list of all medical conditions, approximate date of diagnosis, and the treating physician(s). (8)

6. Give consent for physician(s) and/or designated family members to be contacted if necessary. (9, 10)

7. Accept referral to physician to review possible relationships between anxiety symptoms, illnesses, and medications. (11, 12, 13)

8. Comply with physician-ordered changes in medications, dosages, or administration schedules to alleviate anxiety symptoms. (14, 15)

9. Keep a daily journal of anxiety symptoms to document the frequency and intensity of anxiety symptoms, and specific situations, events, people, thoughts, moods, and behaviors that precede or follow the anxiety symptoms. (16, 17)

10. Identify and clarify the patterns to anxiety precipitants and consequences. (16, 17, 18)

11. List the negative consequences of anxiety symptoms, such as impaired

nomic, motor, cognitive, and hypervigilant.

4. Assist the patient to identify how his/her personal anxiety symptoms fall into clusters.

5. Discuss with the patient the possible etiologies of these symptoms: illnesses (such as endocrine, cardiovascular, respiratory, metabolic, and neurological conditions), prescribed and OTC medications, and maladaptive responses to stressors.

6. Assign the patient to gather specific data on anxiety symptoms for one week through daily recordings of symptom occurrence, time of day, intensity (rated 1 to 10), and duration of symptoms.

7. Assign the patient to produce a list of all prescribed and OTC medications, dosage, and time of day they are taken. If the patient is unable to complete this task, ask that all medication containers be brought to next session.

8. Assign the patient to produce a list of all medical conditions, approximate date of diagnosis, and the treating physician(s).

9. Discuss with the patient the necessity for working with the primary care physician to determine if there may be a biological etiology to the anxiety symptoms.

daily functioning and loss of friends because of social withdrawal, and identify the highest priorities for change. (19)

12. List the apparent positive consequences of anxiety symptoms, such as help and attention from family and friends, and avoidance of stressful situations. (21, 22)

13. Verbalize how the apparent positive consequences eventually lead to negative consequences; make a commitment to learn more constructive ways to achieve positive goals. (20, 22, 23, 24)

14. Identify specific thoughts that precipitate anxiety symptoms. (25, 26)

15. Verbalize a plan to reasonably address rational concerns that generate some anxiety, changing things that can be changed and under the patient's own control, while accepting things that cannot be changed. (27)

16. Replace anxiety-producing thoughts with constructive thoughts. (28, 29)

17. Identify specific stimulus situations, events, or people that precipitate anxiety symptoms. (30)

18. Avoid situations that produce anxiety and in which avoidance does not have long-term negative consequences. (31)

Obtain written consent from the patient to speak with the physician.

10. Discuss with the patient the need or desire to involve designated family members in treatment. If the patient is unable to produce accurate medical information, obtain consent to speak with a family member to get information. If the patient reports that anxiety symptoms are negatively impacting family relationships, obtain permission to contact family member(s).

11. Collect, organize, and analyze data on anxiety symptoms, medical conditions, and medications. If medical etiology seems possible, refer to primary care physician for medical evaluation.

12. Suggest to the primary care physician that if no medical etiology is uncovered (i.e., if anxiety appears to be primarily psychogenic in origin), the first-line treatment approach will be psychotherapeutic rather than pharmacological.

13. Keep the primary care physician informed of the patient's progress in reducing anxiety symptoms, and the desirability of avoiding anxiolytics if possible.

14. Obtain from the physician the ordered changes in medication, dosages, or administration schedules to

19. Use assertiveness to deal constructively with situations that need to be confronted to reduce anxiety. (32)

20. Use adaptive techniques to minimize anxiety. (33)

21. Practice and implement relaxation techniques to reduce anxiety. (34)

22. Identify daily routine activities that have been effective at reducing anxiety in the past. (35)

23. Make lifestyle changes in diet, exercise, and pleasurable habits that will reduce anxiety symptoms. (36)

24. Learn and practice thought and behavioral control methods to minimize and control anxiety symptoms once they have begun. (37, 38)

25. Use cognitive methods to control anxiety symptoms. (39, 40)

26. Cooperate with a substance abuse evaluation to determine the extent of chemical dependence. (41)

27. Eliminate reliance on substances on which a dependence has developed and that have been abused to control anxiety symptoms. (41)

28. Adjust living situation (e.g., move from large home to senior apartment) to reduce environmentally induced stress. (42, 43, 44)

reinforce the patient's compliance with the changes.

15. Review the physician-ordered changes with the patient (and if involved, the family member), making sure that new medications, dosages, and administration schedules are written down in checklist form to facilitate compliance.

16. Develop a simple chart for the patient to record the frequency and intensity (rated 1 to 10) of anxiety symptoms, and to record the precipitating and consequent situations, events, people, thoughts, moods, and behaviors that are associated with anxiety symptoms.

17. Assign the patient to complete anxiety symptom chart on a daily basis.

18. Help the patient to recognize patterns associated with anxiety symptoms: sort out precipitants from consequences; identify the most intense or frequent precipitants; and identify the consequences that help to perpetuate maladaptive patterns.

19. Help the patient understand the negative functional consequences of anxiety (e.g., physical toll on body; negative mood) and current destructive and self-defeating anxiety reduction methods (e.g., social withdrawal, substance depen-

29. Evaluate realistically the need for additional support in performing activities of daily living, and develop a plan to obtain such support to reduce worries about personal inadequacies. (45, 46, 47, 48)

__. _____

_____

__. _____

_____

__. _____

_____

dence, disturbed family or other relationships).

20. Convey optimism to the patient that improved methods of anxiety control will improve daily functioning, relationships, and general quality of life.

21. Assist the patient in identifying current methods of reducing anxiety (e.g., constantly telephoning family, physician, or agencies; making excessive doctors' appointments or going to an emergency room; constant verbalization of worries; social withdrawal) and the apparent positive consequences (e.g., feeling better) from current methods of reducing anxiety.

22. Help the patient understand that some anxiety reduction methods can have apparent immediate positive consequences (e.g., attention, anxiety reduction), but they are maladaptive in the long run (e.g., the physician won't accept calls; friends avoid the patient because of constant worrying; loss of friends due to social withdrawal).

23. Brainstorm with the patient to identify multiple alternative ways of preventing and reducing anxiety without the long-term negative consequences.

24. Help the patient select a few methods of preventing

and reducing anxiety from among his/her brainstorm-generated alternatives.

25. Review the patient's chart of anxiety symptoms and their precipitants to assist him/her in identifying and clarifying thoughts that precipitate anxiety response.

26. Discuss with the patient the extent to which the thoughts reflect a realistic situational appraisal versus an overly negative or catastrophic situational appraisal. Facilitate separation of the rational core concern from the exaggerated, irrational thoughts that generate an excessive and debilitating emotional response.

27. Assign the patient the task of developing a plan to address the rational core concerns (e.g., health management, safety/security issues, welfare of family members or friends, etc.) by changing things that are under his/her control and accepting things that cannot be changed.

28. Challenge thoughts that transform rational concerns into overwhelming and/or unresolvable conflicts; help the patient to identify alternative constructive thoughts.

29. Teach the patient to identify and challenge anxiety-

producing, negative self-talk; assign homework to practice identification of such thoughts, and replacement with constructive thoughts.

30. Review the patient's chart of anxiety symptoms and their precipitants and consequences to help him/her identify specific stimulus situations (e.g., public gatherings where it's hard to hear), events (e.g., doctor's appointments) or people (e.g., upstairs neighbor; daughter-in-law) that precipitate anxiety symptoms.

31. Help the patient determine which situations, events, and people can be constructively avoided (e.g., menacing neighbor; unsafe areas/times of day).

32. Help the patient determine which situations, events, and people can be assertively changed to alleviate anxiety (e.g., discussing conflict openly with a daughter-in-law; asking friends to a quiet dinner at home rather than going to a noisy restaurant where hearing impairment interferes with conversation).

33. Suggest that the patient use adaptive techniques or assistive devices to minimize anxiety (amplifier for one-to-one conversations; cane or walking stick to

reduce fear of falling; reviewing names and faces in photographs before attending a social event to reduce the fear of being embarrassed by memory impairment).

34. Teach the patient relaxation techniques, beginning with deep breathing and proceeding to progressive muscle relaxation and guided imagery. Provide him/her with a personalized audiotape and suggest the purchase of a relaxation videotape if he/she owns a VCR.

35. Assist the patient in identifying the most effective personal stress management techniques (e.g., prayer, walking, baking, telephoning a friend), and encourage daily scheduling of these activities.

36. Review healthy lifestyle issues with the patient (e.g., diet, exercise, caffeine and nicotine consumption, pleasurable activities, etc.) and assist him/her in developing a plan to eliminate anxiety-producers, such as caffeine, and improve general wellness.

37. Teach the patient that a fight-or-flight response is difficult to deactivate once it has begun; that some anxiety symptoms will occur in spite of attempts at relaxation, but that the

response can be minimized by use of cognitive and behavioral control.

38. Help the patient develop a plan of action for specific anxiety situations using behavioral control (e.g., leave the situation if the anxiety becomes overwhelming) and cognitive control (e.g., reassure himself/herself that the anxiety-producing situation will be over in minutes and that the patient is capable of tolerating anxiety for that period).

39. Teach the patient to reframe the experience of anxiety symptoms as a useful, friendly "alert" system that can be escalated with negative self-talk and de-escalated with soothing, positive self-talk.

40. Assist the patient in developing soothing, positive self-talk that effectively de-escalates anxiety response.

41. Evaluate and treat the patient for substance dependence/misuse. (See the Substance Abuse chapter in this *Planner*).

42. Teach the patient the concept of finding a good match between an individual's capacities and the demands of the physical environment. If the physical environment is too demanding for the individual's capacities (e.g., a frail elder taking

care of a large house), the individual can become overwhelmed.

43. Help the patient to determine if the current living situation is appropriate to his/her capacity, or if a change is warranted given the current or anticipated capacity.

44. Assist the patient with psychological components of making a change in the living situation (e.g., thinking about alternatives, choosing, planning, anticipating and grieving losses, adapting, etc.).

45. Help the patient to determine if additional help is needed to accomplish the Activities of Daily Living (ADLs such as eating, bathing, dressing, grooming, toileting, and mobility) or the Instrumental Activities of Daily Living (IADLs such as shopping, transportation, meal preparation, financial matters, etc.).

46. Refer the patient to aging services to obtain additional supports, such as the Area Agency on Aging, faith-based aging services, private geriatric care management, or other community services as available.

47. Discuss the patient's willingness to involve an informal support network (e.g., family members, neighbors,

religious counselors) in providing additional care and services; develop a plan to ask for help.

48. Monitor the patient's anxiety to determine if the addition of supportive ADL and IADL services decreases anxiety.

___. _____

_____

___. _____

_____

___. _____

_____

DIAGNOSTIC SUGGESTIONS

Axis I:

300.01	Panic Disorder without Agoraphobia
300.21	Panic Disorder with Agoraphobia
300.22	Agoraphobia without History of Panic Disorder
300.29	Specific Phobia
300.23	Social Phobia
300.3	Obsessive-Compulsive Disorder
309.81	Posttraumatic Stress Disorder
308.3	Acute Stress Disorder
300.02	Generalized Anxiety Disorder
293.89	Anxiety Disorder Due to (Axis III Disorder)
300.00	Anxiety Disorder NOS
_____	_____
_____	_____

CAREGIVER DISTRESS

BEHAVIORAL DEFINITIONS

1. Feelings of being overwhelmed by daily duties and responsibilities entailed in caring for another.
2. Feelings of despair as care recipient declines physically and/or cognitively.
3. Anger and irritability toward the care recipient.
4. Anxiety about the ability to continue caregiving in the face of continuing or increasing drain on physical, emotional, and financial resources.
5. Low self-esteem caused by the perception of self as an inadequate caregiver.
6. Conflict with other family members over caregiving patterns and responsibilities.
7. Inability to enjoy the potentially satisfying aspects of the caregiving role.
8. Decline in health due to physical and emotional strains of care giving.

___. _____
   _____
___. _____
   _____
___. _____
   _____

LONG-TERM GOALS

1. Cope effectively with physical, emotional, and financial burdens of caregiving while enjoying the rewards of the caregiving role.

2. Maintain care recipient in optimal environment as long as possible.
3. Gain knowledge about care recipient's condition, prognosis, and the probable caregiving challenges ahead.
4. Maximize the use of formal and informal support systems and structures.
5. Avoid the development of serious mental or physical illness.
6. Enhance the safety and well-being of care recipient.
7. Resolve family conflicts regarding caregiving.

—. _____
_____

—. _____
_____

—. _____
_____

SHORT-TERM OBJECTIVES

1. Verbalize the primary sources of stress and distress related to caregiving. (1, 2, 3)

2. Separate sources of distress into more practical *external* areas and more psychological *internal* areas. (4, 5)

3. State priorities for attempting to reduce sources of distress. (6, 7)

4. Verbalize knowledge about the care recipient's condition. (8, 9, 10)

5. Verbalize knowledge about community resources available to caregivers. (10, 15)

6. Demonstrate knowledge about specific practical tasks involved in caregiving (e.g., cooking meals, cleaning

THERAPEUTIC INTERVENTIONS

1. Obtain a caregiving history from the caregiver, including the initial signs and symptoms of dysfunction in the care recipient; if, how, and when a diagnosis was established; current functioning of care recipient; help with caregiving tasks provided by others or through a formal support system (such as homemaker/home health aide services).

2. Instruct the caregiver to make a list of the most stressful aspects of caregiving; reassure the caregiver that nothing is too insignificant or embarrassing to list.

3. Review the most typical sources of stress: grieving the loss of the care recipient

house, bathing and dressing of a frail elder). (10, 14)

7. Explore and identify feelings about providing personal care. (11, 12, 13, 16)

8. Decide whether to provide personal care or to obtain assistance with personal care tasks. (14, 15, 16, 17)

9. Acknowledge the need for *caring for the caregiver,* that is, giving importance to one's own health and well-being. (18, 19, 38)

10. Pursue a professional evaluation of personal physical and/or mental health status as indicated. (20, 21, 22)

11. Cooperate with recommended medical/psychiatric treatments, including taking medications as ordered. (22, 23, 24)

12. Identify and prioritize some opportunities, no matter how modest, for pleasure and relaxation. (25, 26)

13. Engage in and keep a diary of pleasurable activities. (27, 28, 29)

14. Join a support group to provide a continuing opportunity for information sharing and peer support. (30, 31)

15. Explore and resolve feelings of anxiety, grief, and depression related to the changing relationship with the care recipient. (32)

16. Verbalize knowledge of behavior management skills to enhance feelings of self-

as he/she had once been; loss of the caregiver's independence; financial insecurity; anger with others about task distribution; physical health problems; feeling overwhelmed by daily task demands; frustration sparked by the care recipient's behavior, and so forth.

4. Teach the distinction between and interrelatedness of the two basic aspects of caregiving: the practical reality of providing care (e.g., obtaining legal, financial, and/or personal care assistance; changing the physical environment) and the emotional reality of providing care (e.g., managing stress, problem solving, coping with grief, depression, etc.).

5. Review the caregiver's list of stresses, and assist in identifying which stressors are in the practical, objective *external* areas and which are in the emotional, subjective *internal* areas.

6. Assist in rank-ordering the stresses of caregiving, assigning 1 to the least stressful aspects, and 10 to the most stressful aspects.

7. Decide with the patient which of the highest-priority stressors should be tackled first.

8. Ensure that the care recipient has had an appropri-

efficacy in coping with behavioral problems encountered with the care recipient. (33)

17. Practice and implement stress management skills to cope with acutely stressful periods or events. (34)

18. Replace distorted beliefs that exacerbate the stresses of caregiving with realistic thoughts. (19, 35, 36)

19. Family members increase their level of providing care to the care recipient and support to the primary caregiver. (37, 38)

20. Family members attend conjoint sessions to resolve conflicts/issues that may be interfering with providing coordinated care to the care recipient and support to the primary caregiver. (39, 40)

—. _____
   _____

—. _____
   _____

—. _____
   _____

ately thorough diagnostic evaluation. If not, refer to a multidisciplinary geriatric assessment program.

9. Teach the caregiver to compile a list of written questions before the care recipient is taken for physician or specialist visits, and to write down (or have the physician write down) answers.

10. Review how to find more information about the care recipient's condition (e.g., requesting information from the physician; asking for help at the library or bookstore; searching the Web [with some guidance about reliable sources]; contacting disease-specific support groups; calling a local senior helpline, etc.).

11. Encourage open discussion of feelings and uncertainties about providing personal care (e.g., bathing, dressing, grooming, toileting).

12. Reassure that discomfort at providing personal care is a normal reaction, and that it doesn't mean that the caregiver doesn't love the care recipient.

13. Encourage discussion of feelings about the care recipient's increasing dependency, issues of adult/child role reversal, and the mutual uncertainties and opportunities for

misunderstanding as roles are changing.

14. Teach or refer to a source for learning personal care skills.

15. Discuss options for the provision of personal care to the care recipient: informal help from family, friends, and neighbors versus formal help from homemaker/home health agencies.

16. Review emotional (including control and privacy) and financial factors involved in informal versus formal options for the provision of personal care.

17. Assist with processing a decision as to whether to provide personal care or obtain assistance, and from whom.

18. Teach the importance of maintaining caregiver health and well-being; that if the caregiver becomes disabled, the care recipient will suffer. Offer the example of airline protocol for parents to use oxygen first, then help the kids.

19. Encourage ventilation of feelings of guilt surrounding attending to own needs and the belief that the care recipient should come first; counter with a more rational belief that effectiveness requires that the caregiver maintain his/her health and well-being. Give the care-

giver permission to attend to himself/herself.

20. Conduct or refer for full psychological and/or neuropsychological evaluation.

21. Refer for medical, psychiatric, or rehabilitation evaluation.

22. Obtain consent to discuss evaluation results and treatment plans with other professionals.

23. Discuss results of evaluations and recommended care plans with caregiver and consulting professionals.

24. Monitor and follow up on compliance with treatments, adverse drug reactions, and other concerns that should be conveyed to consulting professionals.

25. Assign the caregiver to make a list of all pleasurable activities and events (e.g., special foods, favorite TV programs, visiting family, etc.). Prompt from the *Pleasant Events Schedule* (Teri and Logsdon, 1991), if necessary.

26. Assist the caregiver in rank-ordering the list of pleasant events and activities.

27. Instruct the caregiver to keep a record for one or two weeks of engagement in pleasant activities, recording mood at the time of the activity.

28. Identify one or two activities to add to the schedule or to increase in frequency; specify obstacles to accomplishment and problem-solve resolutions.

29. Monitor the occurrence and frequency of pleasant events, review reasons for successes and solutions to overcoming obstacles; continue increasing levels of pleasure and relaxation.

30. Refer to a peer support group that is either disease-specific or otherwise provides a connection (based on age, religious affiliation, residence, or other common factors).

31. Encourage and monitor regular attendance at, and participation in, peer support group.

32. Process the difficult emotional adjustment to the increasing frailty of the care recipient and loss of "the person I once knew." (See the Grief/Loss Unresolved, Depression, and Anxiety chapters in this *Planner.*)

33. Teach the patient behavior management strategies to cope with the care recipient's difficult behaviors. (See the Aggression/Hostility, Wandering/Way-Finding Deficit, Memory Impairment, and Sexually Inappropriate/Disinhibited Behavior chapters in this *Planner.*)

34. Teach stress management skills of deep muscle relaxation, positive imagery, physical exercise, deep breathing, pleasurable activities, and so forth. (See the Anxiety chapter in this *Planner.*)

35. Identify, discuss, and replace negative and distorted automatic thoughts that could be contributing to caregiver stress (e.g., Replace: "He's doing that to get back at me for what I did to him 20 years ago," with "The disease process makes him do that; it's not directed at me personally." Replace: "I have to stay by his side at all times," with "We both need a break from each other sometimes," etc.).

36. Identify, discuss, and challenge all-or-none thinking that may be exacerbating caregiver stress (e.g., "The only way we can be happy is if he/she fully recovers.").

37. Explore ways that other family members could participate in the caregiving (e.g., staying with the care recipient for a few hours to provide respite; making a meal once a week; sending a videotape of the grandchildren; calling once a week; helping with the finances; paying for yardwork, etc.).

38. Encourage and reinforce caregiver's assertiveness in requesting caregiving assis-

tance from other family members.

39. Lead conjoint family sessions to explore conflicts around caregiving issues and to problem-solve the barriers to coordinated care for the recipient and support for the primary caregiver.

40. If the family is amenable, resolve historical or deeper conflicts that may be interfering with cooperating in providing care, such as childhood rivalries and family roles.

—. _____
   _____
—. _____
   _____
—. _____
   _____

DIAGNOSTIC SUGGESTIONS

Axis I: 296.xx   Major Depressive Disorder
            300.4   Dysthymic Disorder
            311   Depressive Disorder NOS
            300.02   Generalized Anxiety Disorder
            300.00   Anxiety Disorder NOS
            309.xx   Adjustment Disorder
            316   Psychological Factors Affecting Medical Condition

            _____   _____
            _____   _____

COMMUNICATION DEFICITS

BEHAVIORAL DEFINITIONS

1. Difficulty expressing needs and wants to family and staff caregivers.
2. Inability to participate in complex verbal social interaction.
3. Difficulty comprehending instructions or information given by family or staff caregivers.
4. Frustration due to inability to communicate.
5. Behavioral disturbance when frustrated from communication deficit.
6. Embarrassment in social situations due to misperceptions of visual or auditory cues.
7. Social withdrawal due to inability to communicate.
8. Complaints about inability to recall desired words to use in everyday speech.
9. Sudden decline in communication abilities following stroke.
10. Gradual decline in communication abilities associated with progressive dementing disorders.

—. _____

   _____

—. _____

   _____

—. _____

   _____

LONG-TERM GOALS

1. Develop awareness and acceptance of communication deficits.
2. Improve sensory, processing, and expressive aspects of communication to achieve maximum functional capacity.

3. Use devices to compensate for damage to sensorimotor system.
4. Reduce or eliminate frustration and embarrassment caused by communication deficits.
5. Reduce or eliminate behavioral disturbances caused by communication deficits.
6. Reestablish functional interactions with family and staff caregivers in a way that accommodates communication deficits.
7. Re-establish social interactions in a way that accommodates communication deficits.
8. Family and staff caregivers develop realistic expectations about patient's communication abilities and learn to promote functional and satisfying interactions.

—. _____
_____
—. _____
_____
—. _____
_____

SHORT-TERM OBJECTIVES

1. Cooperate with a medical evaluation to assess organic causes of the communication deficit. (1, 2)

2. Comply with a speech/language evaluation of the nature of the communication deficit. (1, 3)

3. Cooperate with a psychological evaluation to assess the role of emotional factors in the communication deficit. (1, 4)

4. Complete a neuropsychological evaluation to assess cognitive status. (1, 5)

5. Participate in a hearing examination to evaluate the

THERAPEUTIC INTERVENTIONS

1. Obtain consent from the patient to participate in multidisciplinary evaluation of communication deficit, including consent to consult with other professionals.

2. Refer the patient for medical evaluation (or obtain records of previous evaluation) to determine whether communication deficit is caused by medical condition (e.g., stroke, Parkinson's disease, Alzheimer's disease, etc.).

3. Refer, or have the physician refer, the patient to a

role of hearing loss in a communication problem. (1, 6)

6. Cooperate with an eye examination to assess loss of visual cues in communication. (1, 7)

7. Verbalize an understanding of the cause(s) of the deficit and the recommendations of the consulting professionals. (8, 9, 10)

8. Family and staff caregivers verbalize an understanding of the cause(s) of the deficit and the recommendations of the professionals. (8, 9, 10)

9. Comply with recommendations for use of adaptive equipment to compensate for hearing loss. (11, 12, 13, 14, 15)

10. Comply with recommendations for use of adaptive equipment to compensate for vision loss. (12, 14, 15, 16, 17)

11. Implement the use of assertiveness skills to ask for clarification of communication. (18)

12. Comply with recommendations for use of adaptive equipment to compensate for poor speech/language production. (12, 14, 15, 19, 20)

13. Communicate simply and with less anxiety and frustration. (19, 20, 21, 22)

14. Family and staff caregivers simplify their level of com-

speech/language therapist for evaluation of the scope and severity of the disorder and for recommendations regarding treatment.

4. Conduct or refer for a psychological evaluation to determine the role of emotional factors (either as a cause or effect) in the communication deficit.

5. Conduct or refer for neuropsychological evaluation to determine the extent to which the communication deficit is associated with general cognitive decline and to identify cognitive strengths and weaknesses that impact on rehabilitation/compensation strategies.

6. Refer, or have the physician refer, the patient for hearing evaluation to identify scope and severity of sensory loss.

7. Refer, or have the physician refer, the patient for vision evaluation to assess extent of loss of visual cues in communication.

8. Integrate findings from all consulting professionals through an interdisciplinary team meeting if possible; if not, integrate findings by reviewing formal and informal reports.

9. Propose an integrated care plan based on the current and projected cognitive status. (Include medical treat-

munication and reduce demands for communication from patient. (9, 22, 23, 24)

15. Family and caregivers adapt their communication to meet the need of the patient rather than insisting on communication modes that result in frustration. (24, 25, 26, 28, 29)

16. Family and staff caregivers attend conjoint sessions to practice communication skills with the patient and to problem-solve remaining difficulties. (25, 28, 29)

17. Family and caregivers use multiple sensory modalities to increase the effectiveness of communication of the patient. (27, 28, 29)

18. Participate in a creative arts program to learn methods of expression that reduce frustration from communication deficit. (30, 36)

19. Participate in physical exercise programs that reduce communication frustration and tension. (31, 36)

20. List pleasurable activities that are not based on language skills. (32)

21. Participate in pleasurable activities that are not based on language skills. (32, 33, 36)

22. Identify and participate in social settings and interactions that are not language-based. (34, 35, 36)

ments, speech/language rehabilitation to maximize functioning, use of compensatory aids, training for family and staff caregivers, and psychotherapy for emotional issues).

10. Meet with the patient, family, and staff caregivers to give feedback on evaluations, propose treatment plan, discuss reactions, and answer questions.

11. Encourage the patient to follow through with recommendations for adaptive devices and services to compensate for hearing loss (hearing aids, adaptive telephone services, closed-captioned television programs, subtitled films, etc.).

12. Help patient problem-solve to overcome physical, financial, and/or psychological barriers to use adaptive devices and services.

13. Use a low-cost, one-on-one personal amplifier (available from an electronics store) in sessions with the patient; encourage the patient to obtain one for personal use in one-on-one conversations.

14. Monitor the patient's compliance with compensatory devices and services; continue to problem-solve and encourage ongoing use.

15. Encourage the family and staff caregivers to monitor

23. Decrease feelings of grief, anger, and sadness that accompany loss of ability to communicate. (37, 38)

—. _____
   _____

—. _____
   _____

—. _____
   _____

and support the use of devices and services (e.g., especially to replace batteries as needed, reinforce device use by patient, provide advice on technology, etc.).

16. Encourage the patient to follow through on recommendations for adaptive devices and services to compensate for vision loss (e.g., cataract surgery, glasses, lenses, magnifying pages, large-type publications, books on tape, reading services, voice and other computer adaptations, etc.).

17. Use increased verbal expression in sessions with the patient to compensate for the inability to see visual/nonverbal cues, especially facial expressions.

18. Teach the patient to assertively ask for clarification when inability to see visual/nonverbal cues or hear adequately interferes with understanding; practice in sessions and instruct the patient and family/staff caregivers to practice at home.

19. Encourage the patient to follow through on recommendations for adaptive devices and services to compensate for speech/language deficits (e.g., speech therapy, sign language, voice synthesizer, word processor, communication board,

motoric communication, etc.).

20. Use simple, direct, brief language with the patient to facilitate understanding; give one instruction at a time; check for understanding after each instruction; teach the family/staff caregivers to do the same.

21. Decrease patient anxiety during episodes of word-finding difficulty by suggesting or filling in words; teach the family/staff caregivers to do same.

22. When asking questions, offer multiple-choice or yes/no options; teach the family/staff caregivers to do the same.

23. Meet with the family/staff caregivers to present the patient's current and expected cognitive status if necessary; explain that brain condition will require the caregivers to assume more burden for effective communication.

24. Teach the family/staff caregivers to lessen communication demands on the patient: by reducing the number/complexity of questions asked, increasing the ability to understand non-verbal cues from the patient, taking an active role with the patient (e.g., reading to him/her).

25. Observe the family/staff caregiver interactions with

the patient to identify areas of stress and dysfunction.

26. Design interventions that facilitate everyday interaction. For example, if the patient has reverted to a primary language and the family/staff caregivers do not speak the patient's primary language, identify key words for communication and make a book or post signs with those key words spelled phonetically and translated.

27. Teach the family/staff caregivers to use multiple modalities to optimize communication. For example, post instructional signs in the environment using both words (NO EXIT) and a pictorial representation (red circle with a line over the picture).

28. Meet with the family/staff caregivers and the patient in conjoint session to practice communication skills; use modeling by the therapist, role-playing by the caregivers and patient, and feedback to improve communication patterns.

29. Have the family/staff caregivers and the patient (if able) brainstorm solutions to remaining communication difficulties.

30. Encourage the patient and caregivers to facilitate patient participation in a creative arts program to

provide for expression of ideas and emotions through drawing, painting, sculpture, and music.

31. Encourage the patient and caregivers to facilitate patient participation in physical activity programs to provide for the release of stress and tension that accompany communication deficit through movement (e.g., dance, aerobics, yoga, etc.).

32. Instruct the patient and staff/family caregivers to develop a list of non-language-based pleasurable activities that the patient enjoys individually and with caregivers (e.g., walking, watching people or birds, playing or watching sports, playing or listening to music, etc.).

33. Assign the patient and caregivers to schedule one non-language-based pleasurable activity per day.

34. Instruct the patient and staff/family caregivers to identify social settings where the language-impaired patient could comfortably participate (e.g., attending church services, stroke support groups, adult day programs, etc.).

35. Assign the patient and caregivers to schedule one social activity every two weeks.

36. Positively reinforce the patient for increased social

and non-language-based activity participation.

37. Help the patient work through grief following loss of communication abilities.

38. Encourage the patient to use therapy sessions to ventilate feelings of frustration, anger, and sadness during the process of adapting to communication deficit.

__. _____

_____

__. _____

_____

__. _____

_____

DIAGNOSTIC SUGGESTIONS

Axis I:	290.xx	Dementia of the Alzheimer's Type or Vascular Dementia
	294.1	Dementia Due to (Head Trauma, Parkinson's Disease, Huntington's Disease, or Axis III Disorder)
	290.10	Dementia Due to Pick's Disease or Creutzfeldt-Jakob Disease
	294.8	Dementia NOS
	291.2	Alcohol-Induced Persisting Dementia
	294.9	Cognitive Disorder NOS
	309.xx	Adjustment Disorder
	293.89	Anxiety Disorder Due to (Axis III Disorder)
	300.02	Generalized Anxiety Disorder
	300.00	Anxiety Disorder NOS
	316	Psychological Factors Affecting Medical Condition
	995.2	Adverse Effects of Medication NOS
	_____	_____
	_____	_____

DECISIONAL INCAPACITY UNRESOLVED

BEHAVIORAL DEFINITIONS

1. A disturbance of consciousness (e.g., delirium) such that the patient appears unable to comprehend decisional issues.
2. Dementia or delirium causes a disturbance in executive functioning, disorientation, and/or a lack of insight into consequences of behavior.
3. A psychotic process causes impaired judgment, illogical thinking, and disturbance of perception.
4. A serious emotional condition (e.g., major depression or mania) compromises decisional capacity.
5. Unable to appropriately participate in specific decisions regarding medical care, such as consenting to withdrawing or withholding treatment, or executing advance directives.
6. Unable to appropriately participate in specific decisions regarding financial affairs, such as withdrawing money from an account, changing beneficiaries, or making charitable donations.
7. Unable to appropriately participate in specific decisions regarding legal affairs, such as signing a contract or getting married.
8. Unable to appropriately participate in specific decisions regarding residential affairs, such as deciding whether to live alone versus in a more supervised setting.
9. Conflict between an individual, family, caregivers, and/or physician about care decisions.
10. Request from family, physician, lawyer, or court for help in determining an individual's capacity to appropriately participate in specific decisions.

—. _____
   _____
—. _____
   _____
—. _____
   _____

LONG-TERM GOALS

1. Exercise the right to make future decisions through execution of advance directives while decisionally capable.
2. Exercise the right to participate in decisions by expressing preferences, even if the final decision is made by a surrogate or proxy decision-maker.
3. Protect self and others from the effects of decisional incapacity by allowing other caring, capable individuals to make decisions.
4. Reduce or eliminate conflict among involved parties when decisions and decision-making capacity are unresolved.

—. _____
   _____
—. _____
   _____
—. _____
   _____

SHORT-TERM OBJECTIVES

1. Describe (or the surrogate describes) in the greatest possible detail the impending decision and all involved parties (patient, family, friends, caregivers, physicians, lawyers). (1)
2. Verbalize an understanding of (or the surrogate under-

THERAPEUTIC INTERVENTIONS

1. Ask the patient (or, if unable, the surrogate) to explain as completely as possible his/her perspective on the current decision-making dilemma: What specific decision is involved? Who is involved? What are the patient's (or others')

stands) the role of the therapist in helping to resolve the decision-making capacity dilemma. (2)

3. Consent (if able) to therapist contact with other involved parties; if unable to consent, the surrogate (family, physician, lawyer) consents. (2, 3, 4)

4. Consent (if able) to participate in medical, psychological, and neuropsychological evaluations of decision-making capacity (or the surrogate consents, or involved parties agree that an evaluation is necessary). (3, 4, 5)

5. Cooperate with the medical evaluation to assess the potential to reverse or stabilize cognition-impairing medical conditions. (4, 5, 6)

6. Verbalize preferences and feelings about the impending decision. (7, 8)

7. Verbalize beliefs, values, and goals about the issues in question. (9, 10, 11)

8. Describe positive or negative personal experiences with issues in question, or experiences with friends or family struggling with similar decisions. (9, 10, 11)

9. Analyze a parallel hypothetical situation and then verbalize preferred outcomes in the hypothetical decision-making situation. (11)

10. Verbalize an understanding of therapist's perspective on

greatest fears and concerns about the current situation?

2. Explain the therapist's role in simple language: clarify the issues; understand and advocate for the patient's perspective; conduct an assessment of the patient's capacity to make decisions; help all parties, including the patient, understand the decision-making process.

3. Explain to the patient (or the surrogate) the limits of confidentiality and the need to work with the physician, family, and others to gain the best outcome.

4. Obtain written consent from the patient (or the surrogate) to discuss issues with other involved parties as necessary (e.g., family, staff, physician, or lawyer).

5. Refer the patient to physician for a medical evaluation of the potential to reverse or stabilize cognition-impairing condition.

6. If the potential exists to improve cognition before an impending decision (e.g., change of residence, surgery) must be made, work with all involved parties to delay decision making until medical condition (e.g., delirium) improves.

7. Ask the patient in simple language (giving multiple-choice or forced-choice—yes/no—if necessary) about the preferred outcome in an

whether the patient is able to clearly articulate values, goals, and preferences; and whether those are consistent with patient's past and with other involved parties. (12, 13)

11. Verbalize preferences and feelings about which of the other involved parties is best able to represent own preferences, values, and goals. (14)

12. Designate surrogate decision-makers. (15)

13. Decide on and implement a strategy to inform all interested parties about surrogacy decision and preferences on advance directives. (16, 17)

14. Cooperate with the lawyer to execute advance directives, legally naming surrogate decision-makers and own preferences for care. (18)

15. Cooperate with assessment of cognitive factors that affect decisional capacity. (19, 20, 21, 29)

16. Cooperate with assessment of mental health factors that affect decisional capacity. (22, 23, 24, 25, 26, 29)

17. Cooperate with assessment of specific capacities in question. (27, 29)

18. Cooperate with treatments that could improve decisional capacity. (5, 6, 25, 26, 28)

impending decision (e.g., Would you rather keep having the transfusions and live, or stop the transfusions and die? Would you rather stay in your home, even if it's not safe, or move to the nursing home where it would be safer?)

8. Help the patient to verbalize fears and concerns about impending decisions, including fears of change, loss, dependency, death or pain, financial worries, concern about being a burden on others, and so forth.

9. Elicit from the patient his/her beliefs, values, and goals that are relevant to the decision at hand (e.g., the importance of autonomy, privacy, altruism, preserving life, not suffering, meaning of life, etc.).

10. Ask the patient about other similar dilemmas in his/her own life or that of friends or family: How was it resolved? How did the patient feel about that resolution? How did that situation help the patient form preferences about the current dilemma? (An example might be a relative whose children withdrew life-sustaining treatment in a terminal case.)

11. Give the patient a hypothetical situation involving a similar decisional dilemma, asking: What should hap-

19. Participate in a conjoint session with involved others to discuss implications of findings on decision-making capacity. (30, 31, 32)

20. Verbalize feelings associated with the current or anticipated loss of decisional control. (33, 34)

21. Verbalize feelings associated with an imminent situation and decisions surrounding it. (35, 36)

—. _____

_____

—. _____

_____

—. _____

_____

pen here? What is best? How will each party feel? Is that OK?

12. Talk with the family, the physician, and the caregivers to get their perspectives on patient's values, goals, and preferences in the past regarding the current situation; elicit family, physician, and caregiver views on impending decision.

13. Determine whether the patient is able to articulate beliefs, values, and preferences; and whether the patient seems consistent, clear, and in harmony with his/her own past values and with those of other involved parties (family members, physicians, etc.).

14. Encourage the patient to speak openly and honestly about which person could be most trusted to carry out the patient's wishes, preferences, and to make unanticipated decisions from the patient's value perspective. Would it make sense to appoint different proxies for different types of decisions (e.g., health care decisions versus financial decisions)?

15. Ask the patient to designate proxy decision-makers.

16. Discuss with the patient the best way to inform all interested parties (family, friends, caregivers, physi-

cian, lawyer) about who will be the designated surrogate decision-makers.

17. Discuss with the patient the clearest way to guide the surrogate decision-maker in the event that he/she will be making decisions: having conjoint sessions to explain the patient's preferences; the patient putting thoughts on paper; the patient and surrogate meeting with a lawyer to explain preferences?

18. Assign the patient and surrogate to meet with a lawyer (private or through aging services) to formalize the advance directives and proxy decision-making appointment(s).

19. Refer for or conduct an assessment of cognitive factors that affect decisional capacity, with sensitivity to educational, cultural/ethnic, language, and sensory effects on performance.

20. Select or recommend tests that will suggest specific diagnoses (such as dementia or delirium); predict everyday functioning (driving, medication compliance); and assess specific abilities relevant to the specific capacity in question (e.g., tests of reasoning and executive function when individuals must use judgment or reason through options).

21. Use *Assessment of Competency and Capacity of the Older Adult: A Practice Guideline for Psychologists* (National Center for Cost Containment, U.S. Dept. of Veterans Affairs, 1997) for general guidance and a review of specific tests.

22. Conduct or refer for a psychological evaluation of mental health factors that could affect decisional capacity, such as depression, anxiety, and characterological styles that might interfere with rational decision making.

23. Administer a self-report scale (e.g., *Geriatric Depression Scale,* Sheikh and Yesavage, 1986) to screen for depression, recognizing that older adults might be hesitant to report psychological distress.

24. Assess whether vegetative signs of depression (sleep, appetite, weight, fatigue) are related to biological illness, medications, pain, or depression.

25. Identify and aggressively treat dementia syndrome due to psychological factors (pseudodementia); delay, if possible, decision-making capacity determination until psychological state improves.

26. Delay decision-making capacity evaluation until

any acute psychotic symptoms are treated.

27. Assess specific capacity, such as Activities of Daily Living (ADLs), Instrumental Activities of Daily Living (IADLs), making treatment decisions, and driving ability.

28. Use findings from medical, psychological, and neuropsychological evaluations to identify and plan treatment for all potentially reversible causes of decisional incapacity.

29. Reevaluate decisional capacity following treatment for reversible conditions.

30. Determine whether the patient's abilities are sufficient to meet the demands of the environment or task(s), recognizing that the environment and/or the task might be modified to compensate for the patient's lack of ability.

31. Determine what strategies are most appropriate for the patient, family members, caregivers, or others to maximize the patient's independent functioning in the future and, if necessary, to compensate for incapacity (through a surrogate, guardianship, etc.)

32. Hold a conjoint session with involved others to discuss implications of the

findings on decision-making capacity.

33. Explore feelings associated with current or anticipated loss of decisional control.

34. Reassure the patient and others that abilities change over time, and that a reevaluation is advisable in the future.

35. Help the patient to understand and express concerns about an imminent situation and decisions about it.

36. Provide support, reassurance, guidance, and comfort to the patient and family as they face the new situation.

—. _____
   _____
—. _____
   _____
—. _____
   _____

DIAGNOSTIC SUGGESTIONS

Axis I:	293.0	Delirium Due to (Axis III Disorder)
	290.xx	Dementia of the Alzheimer's Type or Vascular Dementia
	294.1	Dementia Due to (Head Trauma, Parkinson's Disease, Huntington's Disease, or Axis III Disorder)
	290.10	Dementia Due to Pick's Disease or Creutzfeldt-Jakob Disease
	294.8	Dementia NOS
	291.2	Alcohol-Induced Persisting Dementia
	294.9	Cognitive Disorder NOS
	295.xx	Schizophrenia

297.1	Delusional Disorder
298.9	Psychotic Disorder NOS
296.xx	Major Depressive Disorder
296.xx	Bipolar I Disorder
296.89	Bipolar II Disorder
995.2	Adverse Effects of Medication NOS
_____	_____
_____	_____

DEPRESSION

BEHAVIORAL DEFINITIONS

1. Feeling sad, empty, or irritable much of the time.
2. Loss of interest or pleasure in many usual activities.
3. Vegetative symptoms, including sleep disturbance, appetite disturbance, weight change, observable motor agitation, or retardation.
4. Feeling worthless, helpless, hopeless, guilty, or excessively worried about being a burden to others.
5. Poor concentration, indecisiveness, impaired memory, or other cognitive symptoms.
6. Fatigue or loss of energy.
7. Preoccupation with death (when not appropriate for age or medical condition).
8. Suicidal ideation, plan, or attempt.

__. _____
   _____
   _____
__. _____
   _____
   _____
__. _____
   _____

LONG-TERM GOALS

1. Reduce or eliminate suicidal ideation, plans, or attempts.
2. Reduce or eliminate vegetative symptoms of depression.
3. Improve cognitive functioning related to depression.
4. Increase feelings of vitality and zest.
5. Identify and resolve the underlying causes of depression, elevating mood, and interest/pleasure in life.

6. Reduce negative self-statements and beliefs that can lead to depression.
7. Learn to identify the early warning signs of depressed mood and the preventive actions to take.
8. Practice a healthy lifestyle to prevent the onset of depression.

—. _____
_____

—. _____
_____

—. _____
_____

SHORT-TERM OBJECTIVES

THERAPEUTIC INTERVENTIONS

1. Consent to participate in evaluation and treatment. (1)

2. Verbalize in specific detail problems and complaints related to depression. (2)

3. Verbalize an understanding of the general physical and psychological effects of depression. (3, 4)

4. Verbally identify all of the symptoms representing depression. (5)

5. Complete a self-report assessment to evaluate the severity of depression. (6)

6. Verbalize specific suicidal thoughts, feelings, plans, and actions. (7, 8, 9)

7. Comply with treatment protocol for suicidal ideation. (9)

8. Cooperate with evaluation and treatment of medical causes of depression. (10, 11)

1. Obtain consent to evaluate and treat, including consent to discuss issues with physician(s), and family/staff as needed.

2. Ask the patient to identify specific problems with mood, behavior, thoughts/beliefs, interpersonal issues, and physical health.

3. Teach the patient the depressive symptom clusters: mood disturbance, vegetative signs, cognitive impairment, behavioral signs such as withdrawal or conflicts, negative self-statements and beliefs, and somatic complaints.

4. Teach the patient that even moods and behaviors that don't seem sad (e.g., anger, irritability, interpersonal conflicts, somatic complaints) may reflect an underlying depression.

9. Cooperate with psychiatric evaluation and pharmaco-logical treatment if severity of depression warrants such intervention. (12, 13, 14)

10. Cooperate with neuropsy-chological evaluation of cognitive status. (15)

11. Verbalize an understanding of the multiple conditions subsumed under the term "depression." (16)

12. Identify a personal pattern of depression, in terms of severity, onset, duration, life-time course, possible causes, and so forth. (16, 17, 18)

13. Keep a daily record of mood, rating from 1 to 10 for a minimum of two weeks, not-ing associated behaviors/activities, events, people, and thoughts. (19, 20)

14. Identify whether the symp-toms of depression seem to be primarily related to interpersonal relationships, thoughts/beliefs, behaviors, or stressful events or cir-cumstances. (21)

15. Comply with treatment for interpersonal relationship conflict. (22)

16. Identify specific thoughts that precipitate depressive moods. (23, 24)

17. Replace depression-promoting thoughts with mood-elevating thoughts. (24, 25, 26)

18. Identify specific events/activities that elevate or depress mood. (27, 28)

5. Help the patient identify his/her signs and symptoms of an overt or covert depres-sion.

6. Administer the *Geriatric Depression Scale,* or the *CES-D,* to get a measure of depression severity.

7. Assess the presence/risk of suicidal ideation by asking the patient to share suicidal history, feelings, thoughts, plans, and behaviors.

8. Distinguish carefully between thoughts of death that are age-appropriate; wishing to die that may be disease-state-specific and appropriate; and suicidal ideation that may be a sign of underlying depression, which requires treatment.

9. Follow the protocol for suici-dal ideation if such ideation is present. (See the Suicidal Ideation/Behavior chapter in this *Planner.*)

10. Refer to the physician for an evaluation of medical conditions and medications (prescribed and OTC) that could be causing depression.

11. Discuss the results of the medical evaluation with the physician; support and help monitor the physician's plan to address treatable medical causes for the depression.

12. Assess the severity of the patient's depression through a clinical interview or screening instruments (e.g., *GDS* or *CES-D*).

19. Systematically increase pleasant events and decrease unpleasant events in daily life. (29, 30, 31, 32)

20. Specify details of stressful events that are associated with depressed mood. (33)

21. Express feelings that may be interfering with the ability to cope with change. (34)

22. Accept the reality of the stressful events/circumstances. (35, 36)

23. Identify a successful coping strategy from the past to help with adjustment to current stressful life events/circumstances. (37)

24. Develop a list of possible coping strategies through contact with other supportive resources and select one or more for adoption with the current stressful event. (38, 39)

25. Adopt a coping strategy and adjust as necessary. (40)

26. Monitor and report depressive symptoms, completing self-report assessment on a periodic basis. (41)

27. Identify early warning signs for onset of depressed mood. (42)

28. Develop a plan for early intervention when mood is becoming depressed. (43, 44, 45)

29. Identify sources of pleasure, hope, and meaning. (46)

30. Construct a daily schedule that includes at least one

13. Refer to a geropsychiatrist for an evaluation and pharmacological treatment if depression is too severe for psychotherapeutic treatment.

14. Discuss the results of the psychiatric evaluation with the psychiatrist; support and help monitor the psychiatrist's plan to treat the depression pharmacologically.

15. Conduct or refer for a neuropsychological evaluation to help tailor treatment approach to the patient's cognitive abilities and to determine the existence of a comorbid or prodromal dementia.

16. Teach the patient about different severity levels, causes, and types of depression. Explain that depression can be lifelong, cyclical, or single-episode; it can develop in early, mid, or late life.

17. Teach the patient about causes and concomitants of depression: medical conditions, medication, or medical treatments; genetic or biochemical basis; disturbed interpersonal functioning; learned ways of thinking or behaving; reactions to stressful life events or circumstances.

18. Explore the individual patterns and circumstances surrounding the patient's

pleasurable, future-oriented, and/or meaningful activity each day. (47, 48)

31. Practice a healthy lifestyle to help prevent future depressive episodes. (49)

__. _____
   _____
__. _____
   _____
__. _____
   _____

depression, helping to define the scope and severity of depressive symptoms, and the possible causes of the current episode.

19. Develop a chart for the patient to record daily mood ratings (from 1 to 10), and to record the associated situations, events, people, thoughts, and behaviors.

20. Assign the patient to complete the depression chart on a daily basis.

21. Using the daily recordings, assist the patient with identifying the primary factors in his/her depression: disturbed interpersonal functioning; distorted thoughts/beliefs; self-defeating behaviors; or inadequate skills to cope with stressful events or circumstances.

22. If depression seems primarily related to disturbance in interpersonal areas, follow the protocols in this *Planner* for Loneliness/Interpersonal Deficit, Interpersonal Conflict, Grief/Loss Unresolved, or Life Role Transition.

23. Explore the relationship of negative self-talk ("I'm just a burden to everyone."; "Everyone would be better off if I were dead.") and distorted beliefs ("There's no one like me living here."; "I'd rather never leave my room than have anyone see me in a wheelchair.") to depressed mood.

24. Encourage the patient to distinguish between all-or-none thinking ("Life in a nursing home can't be worth living.") and genuine, nuanced reflection on life's meaning and purpose ("What gives my life meaning at this stage?"); confront the former, encourage the latter.

25. Gently confront unrealistic thinking by suggesting alternative, logical, positive thoughts; use role playing, modeling, and behavioral rehearsal to have the patient practice formulating alternative thoughts in hypothetical situations.

26. Instruct the patient to make a list of all his/her own negative, self-defeating thoughts; assist the patient in replacing each thought with self-enhancing self-talk.

27. Help determine which current activities in daily life the patient considers pleasant and which he/she considers unpleasant.

28. Show the patient how behavior and mood are related: unpleasant events (or an absence of pleasant events) are associated with low mood; pleasant events are associated with better mood.

29. Teach the patient that mood can be improved by increasing pleasant events and

decreasing unpleasant events.

30. Encourage the patient to identify pleasant events that are desirable, but not currently part of a daily routine.

31. Develop a one-week daily schedule with the patient that increases pleasant events, and decreases unpleasant events, making sure to have at least one pleasant event every day.

32. Monitor activities/events and mood through discussion of daily mood/behavior recordings; problem-solve and adjust as necessary.

33. Gently encourage the patient to relate the who, what, when, why, and how details of the stressful event/circumstances.

34. Encourage the patient to ventilate negative feelings that may be interfering with the ability to cope with change (e.g., anger, guilt, sadness, anxiety, helplessness, ambivalence, etc.); the therapist provides comfort and security.

35. Support the patient in recognizing that although the stressful circumstances may be unfair, they are current reality.

36. Help the patient let go of former expectations.

37. Ask the patient to describe other stressful periods in

life, and which coping strategies were successful.

38. Help the patient make a list of all possible coping strategies, such as talking with family and friends, support groups, religion, asking for help, reading books, changing lifestyle, and so forth.

39. Discuss various strategies with the patient, and encourage him/her to adopt one or more explicit coping strategies to help with adjustment to stressful circumstances.

40. Make an explicit plan to adopt coping strategy, implement, monitor, and adjust as necessary.

41. Administer the *Geriatric Depression Scale,* or *CES-D,* on a periodic basis to quantitatively monitor depression severity.

42. Review all depressive episodes with the patient, and help him/her identify early indicators of depression onset.

43. Discuss what interventions the patient or others (family members, staff, friends) might have taken in the past that would have prevented further decline in mood.

44. Discuss what interventions the patient or others could take in the future that would most likely prevent further decline in mood.

45. Help the patient decide on an early intervention plan and take the steps (alerting others, arranging for check-ups, etc.) to ensure that the plan is implemented when necessary.

46. Help the patient to build positive prevention structures into life through the identification of sources of pleasure, hope, and meaning; have the patient list current and potential sources.

47. Assign the patient to fill out a week's schedule with at least one pleasurable (e.g., music concert with a friend), future-oriented (e.g., gardening), and/or meaningful (e.g., volunteering) activity each day.

48. Review satisfaction with the week's activities with the patient, adjust as necessary, and continue to encourage process.

49. Help the patient design a health-promoting lifestyle, including attention to exercise, nutrition, substance use, social support, and intellectual stimulation.

__. _____
_____
__. _____
_____
__. _____
_____

DIAGNOSTIC SUGGESTIONS

Axis I:

296.xx	Major Depressive Disorder
300.4	Dysthymic Disorder
296.89	Bipolar II Disorder
296.xx	Bipolar I Disorder
301.13	Cyclothymic Disorder
311	Depressive Disorder NOS
309.xx	Adjustment Disorder
310.1	Personality Change Due to (Axis III Disorder)
995.2	Adverse Effects of Medication NOS
290.21	Dementia of the Alzheimer's Type, with Depressed Mood
290.43	Vascular Dementia with Depressed Mood
_____	_____
_____	_____

GRIEF/LOSS UNRESOLVED

BEHAVIORAL DEFINITIONS

1. Unresolved bereavement (grief is absent, delayed, excessive, or prolonged) of the death of a spouse, child, parent, pet, or other meaningful relationship.
2. Constant thoughts of the lost loved one to the point of inability to move forward in life to other plans or relationships.
3. Frequent tearfulness, poor concentration, low energy, hopelessness about the future, and pervasive sadness since the loss.
4. Excessive and unreasonable feelings of responsibility for the loss of a significant other, including believing that he/she did not do enough to prevent the person's death.
5. Feelings of guilt about being a survivor when loved one has died.
6. Avoidance of talking about the death of a loved one on anything more than a superficial level.
7. Vegetative symptoms of depression (lack of appetite, weight loss, sleep disturbance, anhedonia, lack of energy caused by the grief reaction).
8. Marked decrease in ability to carry out basic Activities of Daily Living (ADLs) and Instrumental Activities of Daily Living (IADLs) because of debilitating grief.
9. Wishing to die to be with the deceased loved one.
10. Depressive thoughts, feelings, and behaviors associated with a significant personal loss other than the death of a loved one (e.g., loss of a limb through amputation; loss of a home through relocation; loss of physical, cognitive, or verbal functioning through stroke, etc.).
11. Somatic symptoms of fatigue, pains, ache all over, sleeplessness, cardiac symptoms.

—. _____
    _____
—. _____
    _____
—. _____
    _____

LONG-TERM GOALS

1. Resolve feelings of anger, sadness, guilt, and/or abandonment surrounding the loss, and make plans for the future.
2. Improve ADL and IADL functioning.
3. Reduce or eliminate vegetative signs of depression.
4. Adapt to new living patterns while showing acceptance of the loss.
5. Accept the loss and increase social contact with others.
6. Develop a plan for life, renewing old relationships and/or making new ones.

—. _____
    _____
—. _____
    _____
—. _____
    _____

SHORT-TERM OBJECTIVES

1. Report all indicators of unresolved grief/loss, including physical and emotional symptoms, obsessional guilt or self-destructive thoughts, poor daily functioning, and/or poor interpersonal relationships. (1, 2, 3)
2. Verbalize an understanding of the tasks of bereavement,

THERAPEUTIC INTERVENTIONS

1. Explore all current negative grief-related somatic, emotional, social, and spiritual symptoms.
2. Explain that many areas of life can be affected by an unresolved grieving process, and that most people need help (from friends, family, religious counselors, or

and make initial assessment of current place in the process. (2, 3, 4)

3. Keep a daily record of the most frequent and severe symptoms. (5)

4. Report a detailed account of the current symptoms in relationship to the loss (e.g., the date of symptom onset relative to the date of loss, symptom frequency and severity pattern relative to the grieving process, etc.). (4, 5, 6, 7)

5. Comply with a medical evaluation to identify and treat any physical causes of dysfunction. (8, 9)

6. Comply with a psychological evaluation to identify premorbid personality, coping, or interpersonal factors that could be interfering with the bereavement process. (10)

7. Comply with a neuropsychological evaluation to identify cognitive factors (e.g., memory impairment, frontal lobe dysfunction) that could be interfering with the resolution of the bereavement process. (11)

8. Listen to feedback from evaluations and understand that symptom relief will require additional efforts to resolve the grieving process. (12, 13)

9. Agree to proceed with psychotherapy to facilitate the

therapists) getting through the process.

3. Validate the patient's grief, whether the focus is a death (of a person or pet), or a loss of a limb, function, home, or other attachment.

4. Teach the patient the tasks or stages of bereavement: accepting the reality of the loss; experiencing the pain of grief; adjusting to the new life circumstances; reinvesting in new relationships and activities.

5. Ask the patient to keep a daily record of symptoms, noting the time of day, severity, place, people present, thoughts, and other salient facts.

6. Review records with the patient, and together relate the onset of the negative symptoms to the experience of loss and current symptom triggers.

7. Review with the patient whether similar grief symptoms occurred in relation to earlier losses in life; whether depressive symptoms represent a lifelong pattern.

8. Refer the patient to physician for evaluation of any possible physical causes of prolonged depressive symptoms.

9. With the patient's consent, contact the physician for a medical report, and alert the physician that the

grieving process, understanding the usual stages of grieving, and where the problems in resolution may be. (2, 4, 7, 13)

10. Tell all the memories, starting with the positive, of the loved person or object. (14, 15)

11. Integrate negative memories into storytelling as tolerable. (16, 17)

12. Verbalize difficulties in the relationship with the loved one: conflicts, ambivalence, dependency, and so forth. (16, 17, 18, 19)

13. Articulate a balanced perspective of the loved one and the relationship, incorporating both positive and negative aspects. (14, 18, 20, 21)

14. Describe in detail the sequence of events just before, during, and after the death or loss. (22, 23, 24, 26)

15. Verbalize an understanding of the differential impact of the circumstances of death (timeliness, warning, preparation) on the grieving process. (22, 28)

16. Verbalize an understanding of the impact of personality, religion, culture, and family factors on the grieving process. (29)

17. Express feelings of anger, guilt, sadness, anxiety, helplessness, and/or abandonment experienced at the

patient would be using a psychotherapeutic approach to resolve the grieving process.

10. Conduct or refer for a psychological evaluation to identify premorbid personality, coping, or interpersonal factors that could be interfering with the bereavement process.

11. Conduct or refer for a neuropsychological evaluation to identify cognitive factors that could be interfering with the bereavement process.

12. If cognitive deficits are significant, prepare the patient, family, and other care team members for a grieving process that is potentially longer; more repetitive; requires the use of more concrete resolution methods, such as photos, cemetery visits, and repeating religious rituals; and involves more help from the family and caregivers to reinforce the grieving process on a daily basis.

13. Based on evaluations, identify the patient's current stage in the grieving process, barriers to successful completion of the process, and a proposed plan of psychotherapy to work through or around barriers.

14. Ask the patient to talk, at length and in close detail, about the most positive

time of death and/or since the loss. (24, 25, 26)

18. Appraise own role in the loss realistically, without irrational or undue guilt. (20, 24, 25, 27)

19. Verbalize and resolve feelings of anger or guilt that block the grief process. (20, 24, 25, 27)

20. Accept the reality of loss. (26, 27, 30, 31)

21. Tolerate the pain of intense grief without escape or denial. (25, 27, 30, 31)

22. Accept that painful feelings are normal, will be a part of life, but will lessen with time. (25, 27, 30, 32)

23. Develop a personal coping method for tolerating painful feelings: crying alone, prayer, calling a friend/family member, reminiscing with photos, writing in a journal, and so on. (28, 29, 33)

24. Verbalize an expectation of reexperiencing intensified grief on an anniversary date, holidays, and other meaningful times. (34, 35)

25. Discuss the role of spiritual faith in providing consolation and hope during a time of grief. (36, 37)

26. Verbalize a statement of faith that provides hope and support to overcome grief, pain, and loss. (37)

qualities of the lost person or object. Encourage the patient to bring memorabilia (e.g., pictures, gifts, etc.) to the session to facilitate sharing.

15. Allow the patient as much time as necessary to present an idealized version of relationship.

16. Gently acknowledge an introduction of the negative aspects of the relationship: disappointment, conflict, anger, dependency, ambivalence, and so forth.

17. Reinforce to the patient that it is hard to express negative feelings about a lost loved one, but that it is not disloyal.

18. Slowly, as the patient is able, encourage sharing of deepest negative feelings about the lost loved one; stress privacy and confidentiality of the therapeutic setting.

19. Allow the patient to share other thoughts and feelings that may be embarrassing or perceived as disloyal (e.g., sexual attraction to others, relief from the burden of caring for terminally ill spouse, desire to remarry, memories of infidelities, etc.).

20. Help the patient understand that negative thoughts/feelings or relationship difficulties were

27. Participate in family therapy sessions that focus on remembering the deceased, mechanisms of effective coping with the loss, and plans for the future. (38)

28. Realistically appraise post-loss life situation, and determine needs for change. (39, 40)

29. Develop a long-range action plan to adjust to the new situation, including social life, activity patterns, home environment, and so forth. (41)

30. Begin making changes slowly, allowing time for adjustment. (41, 42, 43)

—. _____
   _____
—. _____
   _____
—. _____
   _____

not the cause of the death or loss; challenge irrational guilt.

21. Assist the patient in remembering the loved one in realistic ways, neither idealized nor demonized, so that the patient's participation in the relationship can also be appraised realistically.

22. Encourage the patient to describe in detail the entire sequence of events just before, during, and after the death or loss.

23. Probe the patient for more details on the sights, sounds, smells, and tactile sensations surrounding the loss.

24. Encourage the patient to ventilate feelings that could not be expressed at the time of loss.

25. Provide comfort and security to the patient through the reliving of the loss.

26. Allow the patient to repeat details of the death/loss as much as necessary.

27. Encourage reading books such as *When Bad Things Happen to Good People* (Kushner), *How Can It Be Alright When Everything Is All Wrong?* (Smedes), *Getting to the Other Side of Grief: Overcoming the Loss of a Spouse* (Zonnebelt-Smeenge and DeVries); encourage conversations with others who have suf-

fered losses and/or religious counselors.

28. Discuss with the patient the impact of the mode of death (relative suddenness, warning signs, chronic versus acute illness, levels of pain or discomfort, age at death, time for finishing unfinished business, anticipatory grieving) on his/her grieving process; explain that more time may be necessary under certain conditions.

29. Discuss with the patient the impact of the unique configuration of personality, religion, culture, and family factors that may be impacting the grieving process; adjust the process as necessary (e.g., if culture or family discourages open expression of emotion, find alternative outlets such as a widowed persons group).

30. Support the patient through despair as reality of loss is absorbed. Reinforce this acceptance of reality.

31. Encourage the patient to write a good-bye letter to the deceased, sharing good and bad memories as well as the plan for the future.

32. Reinforce the patient for signs of letting go of the deceased (e.g., reduced preoccupation with thoughts of the deceased, less persistent pining or yearning, decreased feelings of anger and guilt).

33. Explore methods to tolerate and release pain: crying alone or with others; prayer; empty-chair exercise or letter to express thoughts and feelings directly to the deceased; photos for reminiscence; creative arts activities such as music, painting, or sculpture.

34. Discuss ongoing nature of grieving process ("You don't get over it, you just get used to it").

35. Alert the patient to the probability of fresh grief on an anniversary date, birthday, holidays, and other memorable dates; encourage prevention activities (e.g., being with friends/family), but also encourage time to experience feelings.

36. Explore religious belief system of the patient as to it serving as a supportive resource for grief resolution.

37. Reinforce the patient's belief system of love, hope, and compassion, and/or refer to a spiritual leader who can support the patient's faith.

38. Conduct family therapy sessions where the deceased is remembered, loss-coping strategies reviewed, pledges given for mutual support, and plans described for the future.

39. Help the patient assess psychosocial needs (support network, loneliness, intimacy) and practical needs (legal, financial, and housing issues, disposal of spouse's belongings).

40. Encourage the patient to begin considering new opportunities that were not possible before the loss.

41. Assist the patient with assigning priority to needs and opportunities, making the most urgent and/or smallest changes first.

42. Support the patient in the adjustment to a new life, and encourage emotional investment in new people and activities.

43. Provide an emotional safety net for the patient when grief reemerges or during temporary setbacks while developing new roles, skills, and social life.

__. _____

_____

__. _____

_____

__. _____

_____

DIAGNOSTIC SUGGESTIONS

Axis I: 296.xx   Major Depressive Disorder
                300.4   Dysthymic Disorder
                311   Depressive Disorder NOS

308.3	Acute Stress Disorder
300.00	Anxiety Disorder NOS
309.xx	Adjustment Disorder
_____	_____
_____	_____

INTERPERSONAL CONFLICT

BEHAVIORAL DEFINITIONS

1. Frequent or continual arguing with spouse or significant other (e.g., child, parent, caregiver, roommate).
2. Lack of communication with spouse or significant other.
3. Physically and/or verbally abusive behavior toward others.
4. Separation from spouse or significant other due to conflict.
5. Threatened or actual termination of intimate relationship.
6. Inability to establish and maintain meaningful, intimate, interpersonal relationships.
7. A pattern of repeatedly firing caregivers or requesting roommate changes.
8. Inability to adapt successfully to group setting (e.g., adult day care, senior center) due to a pattern of interpersonal conflict.
9. Angry blaming of others for interpersonal conflict.
10. Rude, oppositional, demanding behavior toward friends, family, and/or caregivers.

__. _____
   _____
__. _____
   _____
__. _____
   _____

LONG-TERM GOALS

1. Resolve current conflicts with spouse or significant others.
2. Terminate relationships appropriately as necessary.
3. Eliminate physically or verbally abusive behavior.

4. Understand how personal behavior contributes to interpersonal conflicts.
5. Develop an understanding of depression as both a cause and an effect of conflictual relationships.
6. Learn relationship skills to prevent or resolve interpersonal conflicts.
7. Learn social skills necessary to build healthy, satisfying relationships.
8. Establish mutually satisfying relationships with family, friends, caregivers, and roommates.

—. _____
   _____

—. _____
   _____

—. _____
   _____

SHORT-TERM OBJECTIVES

THERAPEUTIC INTERVENTIONS

1. Verbalize the specific problems in the current conflict, stating the differences between what self and other(s) want. (1, 2)

2. Identify what is gained or lost by perpetuating conflict for both/all parties. (3, 4)

3. Identify three choices to be made as to the future of the conflictual relationship: negotiation, termination, or perpetuation. (5)

4. Acknowledge if one, both, or all parties have a stake in the perpetuating conflict; if so, decide whether to continue participating in the conflict or to terminate the relationship. (5, 6, 7)

1. Ask the patient to identify all the overt and covert problems in the current conflict situation: What are the issues? What are the differences between the patient and other(s)' expectations?

2. Help the patient to identify the severity of the current conflict: Is there abusive language/behavior? Are the parties still communicating? Is termination of the relationship imminent?

3. Explore the meaning of the conflict for the patient and for other(s): Who gains what from the conflict (e.g., power, intimacy, attention)?

5. Make a commitment to achieve conflict resolution versus perpetuation. (7, 8)

6. Verbalize the role of depression as a trigger for and/or a consequence of conflictual behavior. (4, 9, 10)

7. Discuss with other party whether he/she is interested in resolving conflict and, if so, invite to conjoint sessions to facilitate the process. (11, 12)

8. Verbalize own and others' stated willingness to change and the expected impact on conflict resolution. (13, 14, 15)

9. Sensitively terminate relationships in which differences cannot be resolved, in a way that causes the least pain for all parties. (15, 16)

10. Verbalize acceptance of the end of the relationship as a loss and grieve as necessary. (15, 17, 18, 19)

11. Identify concrete behavior, attitude, or situational changes on the part of self and other(s) that would partially or fully satisfy conflicting parties. (20, 21, 22, 23)

12. Verbalize the degree of willingness to make the listed changes of own attitude, behavior, or situation. (24, 25)

13. Ask the other party to delete from the list those changes that he/she is unwilling to make. (24, 26)

Who loses what from the conflict (e.g., love, nurturing, positive pleasures)?

4. Encourage the patient to project the unresolved conflict into the future (one month, six months, one year, five years): What is gained, what is lost, how does it feel?

5. Teach the patient that conflict can be resolved by negotiating changed behaviors or by terminating the relationship, or the conflict can be perpetuated.

6. Help patient reflect on own and others' need to perpetuate conflict.

7. Explain to patient that the therapy process can help to negotiate conflict resolution or to terminate the relationship, but not to perpetuate conflict.

8. Ask patient to commit to resolving conflict through negotiation or termination.

9. Explore the role of depression in the interpersonal conflict: does physical or verbal aggression decrease depressive feelings; are conflictual episodes followed by depressive feelings?

10. Assess whether depression plays a significant role in the conflict. (See the Depression chapter in this *Planner.*)

11. Assign the patient to determine with the other(s)

14. Identify current communication patterns with other(s), for example, willingness to openly discuss differences versus the tendency to avoid or refuse discussion or engage in hostile, angry outbursts, and so forth. (27, 28, 29)

15. Increase assertiveness versus passive-aggressive and/or aggressive communication. (30, 31, 32)

16. Report on the implementation of active listening skills. (33, 34, 35)

17. Directly but calmly express to the other(s) own wishes, willingness to change, and desire for the other(s) to change. (36)

18. Identify all points of agreement and disagreement; emphasize the positive areas. (37)

19. Verbalize a willingness to compromise on remaining areas of conflict. (37, 38)

20. Sign a written action plan to resolve current conflicts. (39)

21. Keep a record of situations that escalate to abuse. (40)

22. Identify the triggers to escalation of conflict into verbally and/or physically abusive behavior. (40, 41)

23. Develop a plan for alternative behaviors when faced with abuse triggers. (42)

24. Sign a written behavioral contract to refrain from ver-

whether conflict resolution should proceed in conjoint or individual sessions.

12. Ask the patient to discuss directly with the other(s) their level of commitment to resolving the conflict.

13. Help the patient identify the extent to which the others' unwillingness to change will limit resolution options.

14. Explore the patient's willingness to change his/her own expectations to negotiate a resolution.

15. If the other(s) decline participation in resolution, and if the patient doesn't accept change options, then prepare the patient to terminate the relationship.

16. Teach the patient to communicate the termination message calmly, using "I" statements, and leaving open the option to renegotiate in the future, to decrease hurt feelings and the likelihood of retribution.

17. Help the patient understand that the end of the relationship is a loss that needs to be grieved.

18. Explore feelings associated with the relationship termination.

19. Help the patient withdraw emotional energy from the terminated relationship and begin to explore new relationships.

bally and/or physically abusive behavior. (43, 44)

25. Identify how the current conflict represents a pattern of interpersonal conflict that is destructively repeated. (45, 46)

26. Verbalize ways in which conflict satisfies personal needs. (47)

27. Identify ways to meet needs more directly. (48)

28. Set aside a specific time each day to devote to communicating calmly and meaningfully with significant others. (49)

29. Increase time spent in mutually satisfying activities with significant others. (50, 51)

__. _____
   _____
__. _____
   _____
__. _____
   _____

20. Assign the patient to write specific changes in his/her own behaviors, attitudes, or situations that would help resolve the conflict.

21. Assign the patient to write specific changes on the part of the other(s) that would help resolve the conflict.

22. Assign the patient to ask the other(s) to write specific changes in their own behaviors, attitudes, or situations that they believe would resolve the conflict.

23. Assign the patient to ask the other(s) to write specific changes on the part of the patient that they believe would help to resolve the conflict.

24. Direct the patient and the other(s) to exchange proposals, but not to discuss them together.

25. Assist the patient in determining whether personal changes listed by himself/herself or the other(s) are realistic: Is the patient able and willing to make such changes? If not, delete from list.

26. Assign the patient to ask the other(s) to determine whether changes on their part listed by themselves and the patient are realistic. If not, delete from list.

27. Explore with the patient current patterns of verbal communication with the

other(s), during both conflictual and nonconflictual
periods.

28. Teach the patient general
communication skills (e.g.,
active listening, assertion,
and nonverbal messages).

29. Assist the patient in identifying the dominant commu-
nication pattern during the
current conflict: open discussion, avoidance of discussion, hostile outbursts.

30. Teach the patient assertiveness skills: "I" messages;
assertive versus aggressive
versus passive statements;
leading with the positive,
etc.

31. Model, role-play, and practice assertion with the
patient.

32. Assign the patient homework to practice assertion
with significant other(s).

33. Teach the patient active listening skills: paying attention, rephrasing, identifying
emotional message, clarifying.

34. Model, role-play, and practice active listening with
the patient.

35. Assign the patient homework to practice active listening with significant
other(s).

36. Direct the patient to continue negotiation of the current conflict resolution
maintaining a calm and
positive atmosphere, mak-

ing "I" statements, asking for the other(s)' perspective, reflecting back statements of others, searching for and stating areas of agreement, and setting ground rules for discussion.

37. Review the remaining change proposals and identify areas of agreements and remaining areas of disagreement, using ground rules and communication skills.

38. Help identify compromises or alternative solutions to remaining areas of disagreements; stress win-win strategies, even if solutions are not perfect.

39. Assist the patient and other(s) to write a behavioral contract with major points of resolution and who is responsible for implementation; get parties to sign the contract.

40. Instruct the patient to keep behavioral monitoring record on a daily basis for one to two weeks, to record the specific people, thoughts, feelings, situations, locations, and times that are associated with abuse; use records to identify triggers.

41. Review with the patient the details of situations that build toward physically/verbally abusive behavior; identify triggers or precipitants that escalate conflict.

42. Help the patient to identify alternative behaviors to verbal and physical abuse in specific situations (e.g., time-outs, self-talk, de-escalation); model and role-play more appropriate behaviors, so that the patient will have them in the behavioral repertoire before the next conflict situation.

43. Write behavioral contract for the patient to refrain from abusive language and behaviors; obtain the patient's commitment to control anger.

44. Assess the patient's control over abuse and potential for more dangerous aggression. (See the Aggression/Hostility chapter in this *Planner.*)

45. Ask the patient to identify how the current conflict is similar to conflicts with other individuals in the past.

46. Assist the patient in identifying the destructive aspects of repeatedly engaging in interpersonal conflict.

47. Assist the patient in identifying the underlying needs or issues that the conflict masks (e.g., firing a caregiver helps to relieve feelings of powerlessness; fighting with a spouse helps to achieve feelings of intimacy; rejection of roommates keeps the family

involved after nursing home placement).

48. Involve the patient in brainstorming more constructive and direct ways of having needs met or issues resolved.

49. Discuss the patient's daily routines and identify a time for at least 15 minutes of attentive, relaxed conversation daily.

50. Instruct the patient to develop a list with significant other(s) of mutually satisfying activities.

51. Assign the patient and significant other to plan for one small mutually satisfying activity every day (e.g., taking a short walk together), one larger activity each week (e.g., going to a movie), and one major activity every six months (e.g., taking a trip).

___. _____
   _____

___. _____
   _____

___. _____
   _____

DIAGNOSTIC SUGGESTIONS

Axis I: 296.xx   Major Depressive Disorder
            300.4   Dysthymic Disorder
            311   Depressive Disorder NOS
            308.3   Acute Stress Disorder
            300.00   Anxiety Disorder NOS
            309.xx   Adjustment Disorder

            _____   _____

            _____   _____

LIFE ROLE TRANSITION

BEHAVIORAL DEFINITIONS

1. Severe and sustained difficulty moving from one life role to another (e.g., retirement, moving to a more supportive or supervised setting, widowhood, new onset disability or chronic illness).
2. Loss of social support network during life role transition.
3. Severe or sustained negative affect associated with life role transition (e.g., anger, fear, grief, anxiety, depression).
4. Loss of self-esteem and/or sense of identity associated with life role transition.
5. Complaints about loss of status or freedom associated with life role transition.
6. Inability to establish positive identity in new role.
7. Inability to establish new social support network in new role.
8. Inability to perceive new role as an opportunity for growth and development.
9. Inadequate skills to cope with life role transition.

—. _____
_____
_____
—. _____
_____
_____
—. _____
_____

LONG-TERM GOALS

1. Resolve feelings of anger, sadness, guilt, and grief associated with loss of former role.
2. Objectively evaluate advantages and disadvantages of the new role.

3. Identify opportunities for growth and development in the new role.
4. Develop coping skills necessary to take advantage of growth opportunities in the new role.
5. Develop social support network suitable for the new role.
6. Adjust sense of identity and self-esteem to incorporate positive aspects of the new role.

—. _____

_____

—. _____

_____

—. _____

_____

SHORT-TERM OBJECTIVES

1. Report all conflicts over transition to the new role, including physical and emotional symptoms, self-deprecating thoughts, loss of identity, and loss of interpersonal relationships. (1, 2, 3)

2. Verbalize an understanding of the tasks of adjustment to a new life role, and make initial assessment of the current place in the process. (2, 3, 4)

3. Comply with a medical evaluation to identify and treat any physical causes of difficulty. (5, 6)

4. Comply with a psychological evaluation to identify premorbid personality, coping, or interpersonal factors that could be interfering with the adjustment process. (7)

THERAPEUTIC INTERVENTIONS

1. Explore all current negative somatic, emotional, social, and existential/spiritual symptoms associated with life role transition.

2. Explain that making life transitions can be extremely difficult, and that many people need help from others getting through the process.

3. Validate the patient's grief due to the loss of the old role, and the sense of confusion while adjusting to a new role.

4. Teach the patient the life role transition adjustment tasks: evaluate what is lost; grieve the loss; see the potential in a new role; learn new skills; develop new relationships; integrate the new role into identity.

5. Comply with a neuropsychological evaluation to identify cognitive factors that could be interfering with adjustment process. (8)

6. Listen to feedback from evaluations and verbalize an understanding that successful transition to a new role will require additional efforts. (9, 10)

7. Identify the current stage of the role transition process and where the problems in resolution may be. (2, 4, 10)

8. Agree to proceed with psychotherapy to facilitate the transition process. (11)

9. Relate positive memories about the role(s) that no longer can be filled. (12, 13)

10. Integrate negative memories into storytelling as tolerable. (14, 15)

11. Verbalize difficulties with former role(s): ambivalence, conflicts, and so forth. (14, 15, 16, 17)

12. Articulate a balanced perspective of the former role, incorporating both positive and negative aspects. (12, 16, 18)

13. Express feelings of anger, guilt, sadness, anxiety, helplessness, and/or betrayal experienced when the old role was ending. (19, 20, 21)

14. Verbalize and resolve feelings of anger, guilt, betrayal, or hurt that block the transition process. (19, 20, 21, 22)

5. Refer the patient to a physician for an evaluation of any possible physical causes of symptoms.

6. With the patient's consent, contact the physician for medical report, and alert the physician that the provider will be using a psychotherapeutic approach to assist the patient in resolving transition process.

7. Conduct or refer for a psychological evaluation to identify premorbid personality, coping, or interpersonal factors that could be interfering with the adjustment process.

8. Conduct or refer for a neuropsychological evaluation to identify cognitive (e.g., memory impairment, frontal lobe dysfunction) factors that could be interfering with the adjustment process.

9. If cognitive deficits are significant, prepare the patient, family, and other care team members for a transition process that is potentially longer, more repetitive, more concrete, and requires more help from others to reinforce the process on a daily basis.

10. Assist the patient in identifying the current stage in the adjustment process and barriers to successful completion of the process.

15. Accept, without escape or denial, the reality of the loss of the former role(s). (21, 22, 23, 24)

16. Accept that pain of loss and anxiety about the future are normal, but will lessen with time as transition proceeds to a new role. (20, 22, 23, 25)

17. Realistically appraise the new role situation, noting both advantages and disadvantages. (26, 27)

18. Accept that the new role, like the old role, will be a mix of positive and negative aspects. (26, 27, 28)

19. Identify the source of feelings of inadequacy in the new role, and specific skills that would improve role functioning. (29, 30)

20. Develop a plan to acquire new skills, either within the psychotherapy process or through other resources. (29, 30, 31, 32)

21. Verbalize an enhanced sense of mastery and self-esteem as new skills are acquired and successfully practiced. (33, 34)

22. Adjust friendship patterns, keeping old friends while expanding social support network as needed for a new role. (35, 36, 37)

23. Verbalize a positive sense of the "new me" and "my new life," understanding continuity with the old role, and

11. Propose a plan of psychotherapy to work through or around barriers. Obtain the patient's commitment to the therapeutic process.

12. Ask the patient to talk in detail about the positive aspects of the roles that are no longer able to be filled. Encourage the patient to bring memorabilia (e.g., awards, pictures, etc.) to a session to facilitate sharing.

13. Allow the patient as much time as necessary to present an idealized version of old roles. Discuss who were the most important people left behind, how life changed, and so forth.

14. Gently introduce negative aspects of the former role: disappointment, conflict, anger, ambivalence, and so forth.

15. Reinforce to the patient that it is hard to express negative feelings about a former role, but that it is not disloyal and does not detract from the importance of the role.

16. Slowly, as the patient is able, encourage the patient's sharing of the deepest negative or conflictual feelings about the former role(s).

17. Allow the patient to share other thoughts and feelings that may be embarrassing or perceived as role failure (e.g., never really enjoyed

growth into the new role. (38, 39, 40)

—. _____
_____

—. _____
_____

—. _____
_____

taking care of the other, always felt secretly insecure at my job).

18. Help the patient to remember the former role(s) in realistic ways, neither idealized nor diminished, so that a realistic sense of self-esteem and core identity are enhanced.

19. Encourage the patient to ventilate feelings that could not be expressed at the time of the ending of the old role.

20. Provide comfort and security to the patient through the reliving of the loss and transition.

21. Allow the patient to repeat details of the loss and change as much as necessary.

22. Encourage the patient to ask, "Why did things have to change? Why me? Why now? Can't I go back?", and to begin to find his/her own answers as a means of resolving negative feelings and accepting reality of the loss.

23. Support the patient through despair as reality and finality of the loss is absorbed. Reinforce this acceptance of reality.

24. Encourage the patient to complete a ritual marking the end of the former role (e.g., giving favorite household items to children, replacing work awards with

charity recognition, giving car to grandchild, etc.).

25. Reinforce the patient for signs of letting go of the old role, and of beginning to explore the new role.

26. Have the patient list positive opportunities in the new situation (e.g., more time to pursue interests, more time with the grandchildren, don't have to cook anymore, etc.).

27. Have the patient list negative and/or frightening aspects of the new situation (e.g., being unknown, loss of status, things are unfamiliar, increased dependency).

28. Explore the similarities and differences between the old and new roles: positive and negative aspects of each; the strategy for each role of maximizing positive and minimizing negative.

29. Discuss specific skill requirements of the new role (e.g., structuring leisure time, financial management, making new friends, managing medical equipment or procedures, etc.).

30. Help the patient identify which skill sets of the new role provoke anxiety due to perceived inadequacy.

31. Help the patient decide appropriate forum to acquire and practice new skills that will facilitate

success in the new role: individual/group therapy, educational classes, library, videos, and so forth.

32. Encourage the patient to make a formal plan for skill acquisition and monitor progress of plan implementation.

33. Review progress of skills acquisition, and reinforce the patient for success in new areas.

34. Reinforce the patient for meeting new demands as challenges and growth opportunities, rather than retreating or avoiding new situations.

35. Help the patient identify what social network would be optimal in the new situation: how many friends, frequency of contact, depth of friendship, and so forth.

36. Ask the patient to identify potential friends, best friends, and so forth, and plan how the relationships could be developed.

37. Support and reinforce the patient during the social network–building process, especially through temporary setbacks.

38. As daily activity patterns and friendship patterns solidify in the new role, ask the patient to reflect on the transition process, specifying what personal strengths have emerged.

39. Discuss the continuity of identity between "my old life" and "my new life," and how the patient's best personal qualities are expressed in both.

40. Help the patient project possible future role transitions, and discuss how the process learned in psychotherapy can be repeated in the future to facilitate change and growth.

—. _____

_____

—. _____

_____

—. _____

_____

DIAGNOSTIC SUGGESTIONS

Axis I: 296.xx   Major Depressive Disorder
300.4   Dysthymic Disorder
311   Depressive Disorder NOS
308.3   Acute Stress Disorder
300.00   Anxiety Disorder NOS
309.xx   Adjustment Disorder
310.1   Personality Change Due to (Axis III Disorder)
_____   _____
_____   _____

LONELINESS/INTERPERSONAL DEFICITS

BEHAVIORAL DEFINITIONS

1. Complaints of loneliness, being all alone, being ignored by family members, having no friends.
2. Complaints of being unable to make friends in a new setting or residence.
3. Depressed mood associated with a poor social network.
4. History of inadequate interpersonal relationships in adulthood.
5. History of disturbed or disrupted family relationships in childhood.
6. Keeps self socially isolated in adult day care, senior center, or residence.
7. Family expresses concern that the patient is socially isolated.
8. Complaints that family doesn't call or visit in spite of evidence to the contrary.
9. Lack of a social network to provide support during difficult life transitions such as retirement, posthospital care, death of a loved one, or relocation.

—. _____
_____
—. _____
_____
—. _____
_____

LONG-TERM GOALS

1. Decrease social isolation.
2. Increase available social network.
3. Resolve depression associated with inadequate social relationships.

4. Understand how unstable social history has led to a pattern of deficient social network.
5. Learn skills for forming and maintaining new friendships.
6. Learn skills for reviving, sustaining, and/or renegotiating family and friend relationships.
7. Learn skills for seeking and maintaining supportive relationships based on mutual need.
8. Achieve greater congruence between family and own perception of contact and support.

—. _____

_____

—. _____

_____

—. _____

_____

SHORT-TERM OBJECTIVES

1. Describe current relationships with family and friends as to frequency and quality of contact. (1, 2, 3)

2. Verbalize distress associated with current relationships, or lack thereof, with friends and family. (4)

3. Verbalize an ideal social network and compare it with the current social network. (5, 6)

4. Reminisce about relationships in the past. (7, 8)

5. Determine whether the pattern of inadequate social relationships is lifelong or due to recent event(s) such as retirement, relocation, or widowhood. (8)

THERAPEUTIC INTERVENTIONS

1. Ask the patient to identify all meaningful current relationships with family and friends.

2. Probe for cut-off or missing relationships from those that would be expected, such as with siblings, parents, children, best friend.

3. Have the patient rate each relationship on a 1-to-5 scale from very satisfying to very unsatisfying; have the patient explicate what makes each relationship satisfying or unsatisfying.

4. Explore feelings associated with existing social network.

5. Instruct the patient to project a specific, ideal relation-

6. Verbalize acceptance of the need for social skill development. (9)

7. Articulate personal goals for social network, possibly including increasing time spent with others, making new friends, rekindling old friendships, and/or developing one or more intimate relationships. (10)

8. Verbalize commitment to work on improving social network, recognizing the benefits of contact with friends and family. (11)

9. Record the frequency, nature, and quality of current social interactions for two weeks. (12)

10. Identify the barriers to pursuing social contacts during moments of loneliness. (13)

11. Specify one or two preliminary steps to overcome barriers to the pursuit of satisfying social contacts; try new approaches for two weeks and record the results. (14, 15, 16)

12. Review progress toward personal goals, and decide with the therapist if this brief intervention is sufficient, or if additional therapeutic support is necessary. (17)

13. List multiple possible alternative ways of increasing social contacts. (18)

14. Identify one or two priority strategies to increase social

ship network: Who would have what kind of contact with what frequency and depth?

6. Have the patient compare an ideal network with current reality, verbalize the contrast, and express feelings associated with the contrast.

7. Engage the patient in a review of past relationships: frequency, size, and intensity of social networks; number and quality of intimate relationships; satisfactions and dissatisfactions about his/her own and others' behaviors in relationships.

8. Use discussion of past and current relationships to assist the patient to determine the cause of inadequate current relationships (i.e., is it a lifelong pattern or the result of recent life changes?).

9. Explain to the patient how social skill development can ameliorate a lifelong pattern of inadequate social network.

10. Help the patient contrast desired social network with past and current real networks; assist with realistic appraisal of possibilities for future interpersonal relationships; integrate discussion to help the patient set realistic and achievable goals.

contacts, noting possible problems that may be encountered and methods to address the potential problems. (19, 20)

15. Review success/failure in increasing social contact and identify remaining barriers. (21)

16. For physical barriers to increased social contact, develop compensatory plan. (22)

17. For psychological barriers to increased social contact, recognize that the therapeutic relationship can be used to understand and practice relationship issues. (23, 24)

18. Identify whether the failure to increase social contact is due to a lack of will to carry out the plan or a lack of skill to carry out the plan. (25)

19. Identify the source of low motivation to carry out the plan for increased social contact. (26)

20. Express positive and negative feelings in a social relationship. (27)

21. Identify specific social skill deficiencies that inhibit implementing a plan for more social contact. (28)

22. Comply with five elements of social skill training. (29)

23. Practice new skills with additional homework assignments. (30)

24. Review progress toward personal goals and deter-

11. Encourage the patient to commit to work toward goals that are within reach; motivate the patient by examples of clinical success from research and case studies.

12. Assign the patient to record two weeks of interpersonal interaction: specify frequency and duration of contact and activities during contact; note any moments of loneliness; rate satisfaction with each social interaction on a scale from 1 to 10; comment on what made the interactions pleasurable or problematic.

13. Review the record of interpersonal contacts as to moments of loneliness or desire for more contact; ask the patient to identify the reasons for not pursuing contact during lonely moments; instruct the patient to make a list of barriers (e.g., time of day, lack of available people, feelings of shyness or anger).

14. Help the patient to brainstorm possible solutions to overcome barriers to more interpersonal contact (e.g., if loneliness is worse at night, find an evening class to attend; if former couple-friends have dropped off since widowhood, identify places to meet new friends).

15. Instruct the patient to identify which one or two possi-

mine if further therapeutic work is necessary; verbalize modified goals/approach. (5, 10, 11, 31)

25. Attend group therapy sessions to further develop social skills. (32)

—. _____
_____

—. _____
_____

—. _____
_____

ble solutions are most feasible and most desirable.

16. Assign homework for the patient to try out new approaches for two weeks and to keep recordings of attempts at new approaches, outcomes, and feelings/ thoughts.

17. Discuss the process and outcome of homework assignments with the patient: determine if the patient was compliant, if progress was made, if the patient seems capable of continuing and extending the process independently or is in need of further support or modification of process.

18. Help the patient brainstorm a large list of ways to increase social contacts (e.g., attending church or senior groups, signing up for an activity or class, calling up old friends or family, writing letters, opening a conversation with someone else in the apartment building, etc.).

19. Work with the patient to identify one or two items from a large brainstorm list to begin increasing social contacts, being careful to pick tasks that can be accomplished with relative ease.

20. Anticipate with the patient possible problems that may be encountered (e.g., confused or negative response

on the phone from a family member); help the patient devise a coping strategy; model and role-play an appropriate reaction.

21. Identify barriers to progress, possibly including failure to carry out plan; nonresponsiveness from others; physical barriers such as hearing/sight/ mobility impairment; psychological barriers such as feelings of anxiety or anger; or skill barriers such as poor communication.

22. Teach the patient methods for compensating for physical barriers to achieving goals of increased social contact: (e.g., attend a group for vision-impaired; purchase personal amplifier; arrange for transportation from Area Agency on Aging, etc.).

23. Discuss with the patient how the therapeutic relationship can serve as a safe laboratory for practicing relationship skills, such as expression of feelings, honest feedback, use of role-playing, modeling, behavioral rehearsal, and so forth.

24. Reassure the patient that good relationship skills can be learned at any age, and are equally important and valuable for women and men.

25. Help the patient to identify whether failure to carry out

plan to increase social contacts is a motivational problem or a skill problem ("don't want to" versus "don't know how").

26. Explore possible sources of low motivation: fear of failure/rejection; feelings of depression, anger, or low self-esteem; distorted beliefs about others' reactions.

27. Encourage the patient to express negative feelings to the therapist without being rejected, to correct distorted beliefs by checking out perceptions with the therapist, to experience positive regard from the therapist, and to express positive feelings toward the therapist without undue anxiety.

28. Assess specific social skills and identify weak areas from among the following: initiating conversations, paying compliments, asking open-ended questions, expressing positive and negative feelings directly and appropriately, improving response style (vocal tone, inflection and pitch, speech latency and fluency), responding to negative comments from others.

29. For each skill deficiency, construct training based on five tasks: provide instruction on skill (e.g., how to use "I" statements to express feelings), model the skill, role-play a scenario using

the skill, give constructive feedback on improving the skill, repeat role-play with modifications, and assign homework to reinforce the use of a new skill.

30. Provide homework assignments to encourage the use of new skills (e.g., making phone calls to friends; introducing himself/herself to a new person; conversing with strangers in a grocery line; inviting someone for coffee; expressing disagreement with another; paying two compliments a day; narrating a story in front of a mirror to learn expressive facial expression and vocal tone; joining a church, hobby, or craft group).

31. Help the patient to appraise whether newly acquired social network and social skills are sufficient, or whether further support is necessary.

32. Refer to group therapy to continue developing interpersonal skills.

__. _____

_____

__. _____

_____

__. _____

_____

DIAGNOSTIC SUGGESTIONS

Axis I:	296.xx	Major Depressive Disorder
	300.4	Dysthymic Disorder
	311	Depressive Disorder NOS
	308.3	Acute Stress Disorder
	300.00	Anxiety Disorder NOS
	309.xx	Adjustment Disorder
	310.1	Personality Change Due to (Axis III Disorder)
	300.23	Social Phobia
	_____	_____
	_____	_____

MANIA/HYPOMANIA

BEHAVIORAL DEFINITIONS

1. Loud, overly friendly social style that oversteps social boundaries and shows poor social judgment (e.g., too trusting and self-disclosing too quickly).
2. Inflated sense of self-esteem and an exaggerated, euphoric belief in capabilities that denies any self-limitations or realistic obstacles but sees others as standing in the way.
3. Racing thoughts and pressured speech.
4. High energy and restlessness.
5. A reduced need for sleep and a denial of emotional or physical pain.
6. A positive personal and/or family history of affective disorder.
7. Verbal and/or physical aggression if wishes are blocked or if requested to comply with policies and procedures considered undesirable.
8. Poor attention span and susceptibility to distraction.
9. Lack of self-discipline and goal-directedness, resulting in unfinished projects.
10. Impulsive behaviors that reflect a lack of recognition of self-defeating consequences (e.g., stealing from others, spending sprees, alcohol abuse, leaving the facility or geographic area without notice or plans, getting in trouble with authority figures).
11. Bizarre dress and/or grooming.

__. _____

_____

__. _____

_____

__. _____

_____

LONG-TERM GOALS

1. Eliminate verbal and/or physical aggression.
2. Increase control over impulses, flighty thinking, and pressured speech.
3. Reduce energy level and reestablish appropriate sleep-wake cycle.
4. Reduce elevated mood and prevent onset of depression.
5. Improve social judgment and social interactions.
6. Cope with guilt and remorse for actions taken while in manic condition.
7. Reestablish positive relationships with family members, friends, and those in residential environment.
8. Accept the need for continued treatment and comply with medication and psychotherapy on a long-term basis.

—. _____
   _____
   _____
—. _____
   _____
   _____
—. _____
   _____

SHORT-TERM OBJECTIVES

1. Cooperate with necessary safety precautions to protect self and others from harm. (1)

2. Cooperate with psychiatric evaluation and recommendations regarding hospitalization. (2, 3, 4)

3. Comply with pharmacological treatment. (2, 3, 5, 35)

4. Cooperate with imposed external limits until behavior and impulses are again under self-control. (6, 7)

5. Terminate self-destructive behaviors. (1, 2, 6, 7, 8, 9)

THERAPEUTIC INTERVENTIONS

1. Evaluate severity of danger to self and others; take immediate safety precautions as needed (removal of weapons, drugs, and alcohol; confinement; medication, etc.).

2. Refer to a psychiatrist for an evaluation of condition, medication, and whether hospitalization is required.

3. Discuss the results of the evaluation with the psychiatrist and develop a joint care plan that mutually supports each other's therapeutic strategies.

6. Verbalize trust in the therapist. (10, 11, 12, 13)

7. Sleep for an extended time during each night, and eliminate daytime naps. (14)

8. Attend therapy sessions for at least 30 minutes, as the ability to attend without agitation and distraction returns. (15)

9. Demonstrate an ability to stay focused in communication with less-pressured speech and flight of ideas. (16, 17)

10. Return to baseline style of dress and grooming. (18)

11. Verbalize awareness of mood swing pattern. (19, 20)

12. Conduct mood self-monitoring and report symptoms of elation or depression to the therapist and the psychiatrist. (21, 22)

13. Identify early warning signs of mood swings. (23)

14. Identify stressors that trigger mood swings, and verbalize a plan to cope with or avoid these stressors. (24)

15. Acknowledge the impulsive behaviors that occurred during the manic episode. (25, 26, 27)

16. Identify the negative consequences of the impulsive behaviors that occurred during the manic episode. (28, 29, 30)

4. Arrange for or support hospitalization if the patient is judged to be potentially harmful to himself/herself or others, or unable to care for his/her own basic needs.

5. Obtain information from the psychiatrist regarding the ordered medication(s), dosages, and administration schedules to encourage and reinforce the patient's compliance.

6. Teach caregivers, staff, and family about the illness and the importance of providing limits for external control while the patient is in a manic/hypomanic episode.

7. Help all involved to problem-solve how to impose limits for safety without exacerbating the patient's hostility and aggression (usually in the most indirect, unobtrusive, and/or least confrontational way).

8. Review with caregivers, staff, and family the ways in which the patient is being self-destructive and remove methods (take away car keys, credit cards, cash, etc.).

9. Teach involved others to provide multiple substitute activities and projects for the patient to use the excessive energy without being self-destructive.

10. See the patient in frequent, brief sessions, as tolerable for the patient's current dis-

17. Use therapy sessions to verbalize the patient's own social judgment and accept feedback from the therapist. (31)

18. Develop a plan to repair social relationships that were damaged during the manic episode. (29, 30, 32)

19. Verbalize guilt and remorse for actions taken while in the manic condition. (28, 32, 33)

20. Assume responsibility for actions while accepting the force of mental illness. (25, 26, 34, 35)

21. Express remorse and offer reparations to those who were harmed emotionally, physically, or financially during manic episode. (32, 36)

22. Share information with affected others (staff in residential facility, family, friends, in-home caregivers) about this mental illness, and ask them to contact the treating professionals should they see early warning signs of a new episode. (37)

23. Verbalize an acceptance of the necessity for continued medical treatment and monitoring for manic/hypomanic states. (35, 38)

24. Join a support group for those suffering from manic/hypomanic conditions. (39)

tractibility and agitation level.

11. If necessary/possible, see the patient in a context where physical movement is possible: walking outside or in a hallway together.

12. Avoid direct confrontations with the patient, but provide a calm, reasoned presence.

13. Reassure the patient that the therapist can be trusted not to reject or abandon the patient.

14. Instruct staff/family caregivers to guide the patient back onto a regular sleep-wake cycle as the medication begins to take effect by discouraging daytime naps and using nighttime sleep compression techniques. (See the Sleep Disturbance chapter in this *Planner*.)

15. Extend therapy sessions as the patient is able to attend for longer periods of time, gradually increasing to 30 minutes.

16. Provide structure and focus to the patient's thoughts and actions within sessions, and help the patient to begin focusing on reestablishing plans and routines in daily life.

17. Verbally reinforce slower speech and a more deliberate thought process.

18. Encourage and reinforce appropriate dress and

25. Become an advocate for those with mental illness, moving from an identity as a victim to an empowered survivor. (40)

—. _____

_____

—. _____

_____

—. _____

_____

grooming; teach staff/family caregivers to do same.

19. Review lifelong course of illness with the patient and family and how this episode fits into the pattern.

20. Help the patient identify changes in episodic pattern: whether there is evidence that cycles are shortening with age, or development of a rapid cycling pattern.

21. Teach the patient to chart mood, rating from 1 to 10, and to keep daily mood diaries for self-monitoring.

22. Instruct the patient to share mood diaries with the therapist and the psychiatrist, discussing any major changes in mood.

23. Help the patient identify personal indicators that distinguish between a pleasant or euthymic mood versus the onset of mania/hypomania and between a blue day versus the onset of depression.

24. Assign the patient to identify, with the help of family, stressors that have been associated with the onset of mood disturbance throughout his/her lifetime, and ways to avoid or manage those stressors.

25. Confront the patient with an accounting of the impulsive behaviors that occurred during the episode; gently but firmly get the patient to

acknowledge the reality of negative behaviors.

26. In conjoint sessions, have staff/family caregivers describe impulsive, self-destructive behaviors they witnessed during the episode, and their feelings during the interactions.

27. Reduce the patient's defensiveness and guilt to the point at which the patient can acknowledge the extent of negative, dangerous, and hurtful behaviors that occurred during the episode.

28. Instruct the patient to list all the events and behaviors that have been recounted, and for each one, to describe the negative consequences—concrete and emotional—for himself/herself and others.

29. Process the patient's list of the negative consequences with the affected others, having them add their views of the consequences.

30. Continue working with the patient and affected others, until the patient accepts the reality of the negative consequences of behaviors during the episode.

31. Teach the patient to check his/her own judgment about social interactions and consequences with the therapist; slowly transfer the checking of social judgment to trusted family members and friends.

32. Review the list of impulsive behaviors and consequences with the patient, and develop a plan to repair damaged social relationships, including apologies, conjoint therapy sessions, restitution of property, offers to pay medical bills, and so forth.

33. Explore the patient's deepest feelings of guilt, remorse, inadequacy, fear, and insecurity, conveying warmth and unconditional acceptance.

34. Help the patient understand the delicate balance between the need to assume responsibility for actions while simultaneously acknowledging the power of mental illness.

35. Encourage the patient's commitment to struggling with mental illness by maintaining compliance with medication and mood/behavior self-monitoring.

36. Assist (through conjoint sessions) and support the patient's implementation of the plan to repair social relationships.

37. Instruct staff/family caregivers to contact the treating professionals with any early warning signs of mood upswing or downturn.

38. Provide the patient with reading material about this mental illness and those

who have overcome it with ongoing pharmacological and psychotherapeutic help.

39. Encourage the patient to join a support group for those suffering from Bipolar Disorder or a general support group for chronic mental illness.

40. Encourage the patient to join an association or advocacy group for Bipolar Disorder and/or chronic mental illness, and to become involved in its activities.

—. _____
   _____

—. _____
   _____

—. _____
   _____

DIAGNOSTIC SUGGESTIONS

Axis I:	296.xx	Bipolar I Disorder
	296.89	Bipolar II Disorder
	301.13	Cyclothymic Disorder
	295.70	Schizoaffective Disorder
	296.80	Bipolar Disorder NOS
	310.1	Personality Change Due to (Axis III Disorder)
	_____	_____
	_____	_____

MEDICAL/MEDICATION
ISSUES UNRESOLVED

BEHAVIORAL DEFINITIONS

1. A diagnosed serious medical condition that needs attention and has an impact on daily living (e.g., high blood pressure, heart disease, cancer, cirrhosis, diabetes, thyroid conditions, arthritis, etc.).
2. Pain, fatigue, a general feeling of ill health, confusion, falls, or other symptoms of a serious medical condition that has not been diagnosed, or is not under a physician's care.
3. Noncompliance with prescribed treatment for a medical condition.
4. Psychological or behavioral factors that influence the course of the medical condition.
5. Poor compliance with medications because of unwanted side effects or cognitive inability to correctly follow directions for the administration of medications.
6. Evidence of adverse drug reactions (ADRs), such as dizziness, mental confusion, hallucinations, depression, and so forth.
7. Prescriptions for more than five medications and/or additional over-the-counter medications and/or poor use of medication reminder systems.
8. Use of multiple pharmacies and/or prescribing physicians without professional awareness or medication coordination.

__. _____
_____
__. _____
_____
__. _____
_____

LONG-TERM GOALS

1. Seek/accept appropriate medical care for physical condition(s).
2. Comply with prescribed treatment for medical condition(s).
3. Address psychological or behavioral factors that may be interfering with appropriate use of medical services or otherwise negatively affecting health outcomes.
4. Receive coordinated medical and pharmaceutical care.
5. Comply with medications as prescribed, and report evidence of ADRs to the prescribing physician.
6. Have medications reviewed on a regular basis to simplify prescription schedules or to search for opportunities to decrease the number and dosage of medications.

—. _____

_____

—. _____

_____

—. _____

_____

SHORT-TERM OBJECTIVES

1. Verbalize all current symptoms, including physical, cognitive, emotional, and behavioral. (1, 2)

2. Compile a list of all diagnosed medical conditions, approximate date of diagnosis, and the treating professionals. (3, 4)

3. Compile a list of all prescribed and over-the-counter medications and regimens, dosages, and times of the day that they are taken. (5, 6)

4. Give written consent for the physician(s) and/or desig-

THERAPEUTIC INTERVENTIONS

1. Assign the patient to verbalize or list all specific physical, cognitive, emotional, and behavioral symptoms.

2. Help the patient rank-order the symptoms on the basis of how disturbing they are and cluster the symptoms into physical, cognitive, emotional, and behavioral categories.

3. Assign the patient to produce a list of all medical conditions, approximate date of diagnosis, the treating professionals, and their phone numbers.

nated family/staff member to be contacted if necessary. (7, 8)

5. Verbalize an understanding of the complex, interactive relationship between the psychological and physical aspects of human functioning (mind/body interrelationships). (9, 10)

6. Accept responsibility for caring for personal health, or if unable, designate a family or staff member who will be responsible for coordinating care. (11, 12, 13)

7. Verbalize an understanding of, or find a family or staff member, or a care manager who understands the benefits and limitations of the health insurance plan. (14, 15, 16)

8. Identify the personal and/or systemic barriers to appropriate or causes for inappropriate medical care. (17, 18)

9. Verbalize an understanding that depression, hopelessness, anxiety, and/or substance misuse can lead to giving up on personal health, or making medical conditions worsen. (19, 20)

10. Agree to comply with treatment for psychological conditions that interfere with the appropriate treatment of medical conditions. (21)

11. Verbalize an increased knowledge of medical conditions and medications. (22, 23, 24, 25)

4. Instruct the patient to list nonphysician health care providers (nutritionists, chiropractors, herbalists, etc.), with phone numbers, frequency of contact, and recommended regimens.

5. Assign the patient to produce a list of all prescribed and over-the-counter medications and preparations, dosages, and time of the day that they are taken.

6. If the patient is unable to complete a medication list, ask that all medications and preparation containers be brought to the next session or that a family/staff member assist.

7. Discuss with the patient the necessity for working with all treating professionals to ensure coordination of care. Obtain written consent for release of information.

8. Discuss with the patient the need to involve a family or staff member in coordinating treatment or providing information. Obtain written consent to speak with a family or staff member.

9. Teach the patient the multiple possible pathways between physical and psychological conditions: causality in either direction, comorbidity, interference with motivation, and so forth.

10. Explain the importance of working on both physical

12. Record and communicate, or have a family/staff member record and communicate medical data to health care providers by sending copies to all treating professionals; use a formal care manager if available/necessary. (16, 26, 27, 28)

13. Request all physician specialists to send reports to the primary care physician. (29)

14. Coordinate medication usage by using only one pharmacy and asking the pharmacist to review all medications for appropriateness and possible interactions. (24, 30)

15. Report all possible ADR symptoms to both the pharmacist and the prescribing physician. (24, 25, 27, 28, 29)

16. Ask the pharmacist to communicate with the prescribing physician if changes are recommended. (24, 30, 31)

17. Have a family or staff member administer pill counts weekly to determine compliance with the regimen. (32, 33, 34)

18. Use medication reminders to improve compliance with prescribed regimen. (35)

19. Arrange for medication administration by a family or staff member. (33, 34, 36, 37)

20. Verbalize the right and responsibility to be

and psychological fronts simultaneously, as the progress in one area will have a positive impact in the other.

11. Discuss with the patient the importance of taking personal or family responsibility for health care in today's system because of the structure of health care delivery.

12. Discuss with the patient whether there is a family member or staff person who should be involved in coordinating health care.

13. If necessary, designate a surrogate health care decision-maker. (See the Decisional Incapacity chapter in this *Planner.*)

14. Assign the patient to locate and read information on personal health insurance benefits. Obtain help as needed from a family or staff member.

15. If confusion persists regarding insurance benefits, assign the patient, or a family/staff member to contact the insurance carrier representative for further explanation.

16. If confusion persists regarding health insurance benefits and requirements, suggest that the patient use a care manager (through the Area Agency on Aging, faith-based, or private) to help coordinate insurance and health care.

assertive with health care providers; learn assertiveness skills. (11, 38, 39)

21. Demonstrate assertiveness with treating professionals about personal health care. (38, 39, 40)

22. Ask questions of the family, staff member, or formal care manager, to help understand and obtain the best medical benefits and insurance options. (16, 41)

23. Arrange for continued medication monitoring by the pharmacist and the physicians to reduce polypharmacy and the risk of ADRs, and to simplify medication administration schedules. (42)

—. _____
   _____
—. _____
   _____
—. _____
   _____

17. Explore with the patient (and family/staff if necessary) the causes for inappropriate medical care.

18. Determine with the patient whether the cause for inappropriate medical care is personal (depression, anxiety, passivity, substance abuse, poor memory, lack of medical knowledge) or systemic (poor treatment coordination, inadequate financial resources).

19. Explain the negative impact on health from depression, hopelessness, anxiety, and/or substance misuse.

20. Teach the patient that emotional/behavioral dysfunctions are treatable conditions that will improve, and as they improve, motivation for good health care will improve, and physical well-being will improve.

21. Treat the emotional/behavioral conditions that interfere with medical care. (See the Depression, Anxiety, and Substance Dependence/Misuse chapters in this *Planner*.)

22. Help the patient to identify sources for information about his/her specific medical conditions: library, bookstore, reliable sources on the Internet, disease-specific organizations.

23. Loan the patient a medical or medication book (see Bibliotherapy suggestions). Put information in perspective to alleviate unnecessary anxiety.

24. Encourage the patient to talk with a local pharmacist at a relatively quiet and private time about medication effects, interactions, and side effects.

25. Encourage the patient to call the treating professional(s) with specific questions about condition(s) or medications.

26. Help the patient establish a personal medical record, with initial entries reflecting gathered data on medical conditions and medications.

27. Encourage the patient to keep records of appointments, emergent conditions, medication reactions or changes, health regimens, resolved conditions, and so forth.

28. Instruct the patient, or care manager, to copy medical information and send it to the primary care physician and others as appropriate as a method to improve coordination of care.

29. Instruct the patient to request that any treating professional send written reports to the primary care physician to improve coordination of care.

30. Determine if the patient is using multiple pharmacies; insist that all prescriptions be filled by a single pharmacist to decrease the possibility of adverse drug reactions (ADRs).

31. If the pharmacist suggests medication changes, instruct the patient to call the prescribing physician, but also to ask the pharmacist to call the prescribing physician to increase impact.

32. Obtain consent from the patient for a pill count procedure.

33. Instruct a family/staff member to count pills at the beginning of the week, to calculate what should be left after a week if the regimen is followed, and then count at the end of the week.

34. Ask a family/staff member to report on weekly pill count, noting whether there is a discrepancy that indicates noncompliance.

35. Discuss medication compliance packaging and reminder systems with the pharmacist; identify the best system to address noncompliance issues and implement.

36. Ask the patient to choose a family member or staff member (within staff scope of practice) to administer/supervise medications.

37. Review, or have the pharmacist or treating professionals review medications, dosages, schedules, and ADRs with a family/staff member to improve medication compliance.

38. Use modeling, role-playing, and behavioral rehearsal to teach the patient basic assertiveness skills (e.g., "I" statements, active listening, questions for clarification, etc.).

39. Teach the patient specific assertiveness skills for health care: writing down questions beforehand, refusing to be hurried through appointments, taking an assertive support person to appointments, asking the physician to write down instructions.

40. Ask the patient to report on interactions with health care providers, and whether assertiveness was used; provide encouragement and practice.

41. Instruct the patient to ask a family/staff member or a care manager to help decipher current and potential health benefits and options.

42. Instruct the patient or a family/staff member to have the pharmacist and the treating professional regularly review all medications to look for opportunities to decrease dosage, eliminate medications, or simplify

schedules of medication
administration.

—.   _____
     _____
—.   _____
     _____
—.   _____
     _____

DIAGNOSTIC SUGGESTIONS

Axis I: 293.0   Delirium Due to (Axis III Disorder)
              310.1   Personality Change Due to (Axis III Disorder)
              293.9   Mental Disorder NOS Due to (Axis III
                         Disorder)
              296.xx   Major Depressive Disorder
              300.4   Dysthymic Disorder
              311   Depressive Disorder NOS
              300.02   Generalized Anxiety Disorder
              293.89   Anxiety Disorder Due to (Axis III Disorder)
              300.00   Anxiety Disorder NOS
              307.xx   Pain Disorder
              995.2   Adverse Effects of Medication NOS

              _____   _____
              _____   _____

MEMORY IMPAIRMENT

BEHAVIORAL DEFINITIONS

1. Reduced ability to recall prior events or conversation.
2. Complaints of poor memory.
3. Forgetfulness interferes with Activities of Daily Living (e.g., missed appointments, medication regimen mismanaged, confusion over financial affairs, food left to burn on the stove, etc.).
4. Social withdrawal due to embarrassment about poor memory.
5. Feelings of frustration, sadness, and insecurity due to realization of memory impairment and its ramifications.

—. _____
_____
—. _____
_____
—. _____
_____

LONG-TERM GOALS

1. Use compensatory strategies for nonreversible components of memory loss.
2. Improve memory functioning by resolving causative factors related to medication side effects, mental illness effects, and/or a reversible medical condition.
3. Resolve negative emotional consequences associated with the impact of memory loss on Activities of Daily Living.
4. Accept and understand the extent of and causes for the memory loss.
5. Accept and adjust to the possible need for an increased level of supervision.

6. Protect and enhance personal autonomy, given the current and projected impairment.

—. _____
   _____

—. _____
   _____

—. _____
   _____

SHORT-TERM OBJECTIVES

1. Complete neuropsychological and medical evaluation. (1, 2, 3)

2. Complete treatment for confounding or coexisting depression, anxiety, medical conditions, and/or adverse drug reactions. (4, 5)

3. Verbalize an understanding and acceptance of causes for and extent of memory loss. (6)

4. Verbalize preferences as to what extent and how to involve which family members and others in the care and care planning. (7)

5. Family members/caregivers express an understanding of the causes for an extent of the memory impairment. (8)

6. Family members/caregivers implement strategies to support the patient in coping with memory loss. (9, 17)

7. Family members/caregivers reassure the patient that

THERAPEUTIC INTERVENTIONS

1. Refer and arrange for the patient to have neuropsychological and medical evaluations to determine the nature, severity, and cause of the memory deficits.

2. Conduct or refer for appropriate neuropsychological (e.g., WAIS-III, WMS-R, California Verbal Learning Test, Memory Assessment Scales, etc.) and psychological evaluations to determine the nature and severity of the memory deficits and to determine the possible contribution of depression and/or anxiety to memory complaint or performance deficit.

3. Discuss the results of the evaluations and the plan for addressing treatable medical and psychological causes for the memory deficits with the physician.

4. Develop appropriate psychological treatment objectives

they will be in personal and/or telephone contact with him/her to provide support and reminders on a mutually agreeable schedule. (10)

8. Family members/caregivers practice and implement calm, kind, nonalarming repetition of informational reminders to the patient. (11)

9. Verbalize feelings of frustration, sadness, embarrassment, and/or insecurity that result from the realization of memory loss. (12)

10. Verbalize a sense of peace of mind that results from plans for and implementation of coping strategies and caregiver support. (10, 11, 12, 13)

11. Carry a note pad and pen and the patient can write himself/herself reminder notes (if effective, not frustrating). (14, 24)

12. Use a chalkboard or post-it notes in the living environment for the patient to write reminders to himself/herself if effective. (15, 24)

13. Develop and implement a daily checkoff routine that is written down and posted in the living area. (16, 24)

14. Take medications and keep appointments according to a written, posted schedule, using an organizer as necessary. (16, 17, 24)

for the memory deficit based on the neuropsychological and medical evaluations.

5. Develop a plan to address the reversible psychological causes for the memory loss. (See the Depression, Anxiety, and/or Substance Dependence/Misuse chapters in this *Planner.*)

6. Discuss the results of the neuropsychological and psychological evaluations with the patient, explaining the causes for and extent of memory loss; help the physician clarify medical results as necessary.

7. Discuss current and expected preferences (e.g., living arrangements, surrogate decision-makers, etc.), competencies (e.g., decision making), and goals. Elicit preferences about family/caregiver involvement.

8. With the patient's consent, and in consultation with the physician, meet with the family members/caregivers to disclose the results of the evaluations, explaining the causes for and extent of memory loss.

9. Teach the family members/caregivers coping strategies (e.g., write notes and avoid reliance on verbal channels of communication; install a board in the patient's living area for posting reminder messages; make regular, mutually agreed-upon con-

15. Develop and post labels for locating items needed for activities of daily living. (18, 24)

16. If still mildly impaired and motivated to do so, report accurate identification of the day, date, and names of family members/caregivers. (19, 20, 24)

17. Complete memory-enhancing word puzzles every day. (21, 24)

18. Perform the cognitively stimulating activity of playing along with TV game shows (e.g., *Jeopardy, Wheel of Fortune*) every day. (22, 24)

19. Report the results of using the memory-enhancing techniques of association and imagery. (23, 24)

20. Report implementation of pleasant social contacts with friends, relatives, and caregivers. (25)

21. Verbalize an understanding of a possible future course for memory deficits. (26)

22. Verbalize acceptance of the need for increased daily supervision and cooperate with an appropriate referral for obtaining such services. (27)

__. _____
   _____
__. _____
   _____
__. _____
   _____

tact with the patient to check on his/her status, etc.) to help the patient with memory loss.

10. Encourage the family/caregivers to reassure the patient of predictable contact to reduce his/her feelings of insecurity.

11. Use role-playing and modeling to teach the family/caregivers to respond calmly and kindly to the patient's instances of memory loss rather than with frustration, anger, or alarm. Teach validation of feelings rather than challenge of facts.

12. Discuss emotional reaction to diagnosis and prognosis for memory impairment, including grieving the possible further loss of function and control.

13. Assist the patient to regain a sense of control by discussing and arranging for him/her to write advance directives for care.

14. Assign the patient to write down important messages to himself/herself as a means of reducing forgetting. Advise the patient to stop if it is ineffective or frustrating.

15. Encourage the patient to post reminders to himself/herself on a board or with post-it notes regarding things he/she needs to remember. Advise the patient to stop if it is ineffective or frustrating.

16. Develop a daily schedule that includes medication schedule. Encourage the patient to post the schedule at a key place in the living environment and to check off behaviors as they are implemented. Advise the patient to stop if it is ineffective or frustrating.

17. Direct the patient in the use of a medication organizer that contains the medications for each time of administration each day. Urge the family members/caregivers to oversee this process if necessary.

18. Develop a list of labels to be posted in the patient's living environment that provides cues as to the location of things needed for daily living (e.g., food items, medications, personal care products, etc.)

19. Encourage the patient to hang a calendar in a prominent place in the living environment and to cross off days before he/she goes to sleep and circle the new day as he/she gets up in the morning. Do not persist if the patient cannot learn the cross off/circle routine.

20. Encourage the patient to label photographs of friends, family members/caregivers with names and post them for easy reference or review.

21. Assign the patient memory-enhancing exercises, such

as crossword or other word puzzles found in books or daily newspapers.

22. Assign the patient cognitively stimulating activities, such as playing along with TV game shows (such as *Jeopardy* or *Wheel of Fortune*), playing challenging card games, or computer activities.

23. Assign the patient to practice memory techniques, such as association (associating names with striking images or rhymes), categorization (remembering things by grouping them), or first-letter mnemonics (such as remembering the Great Lakes as HOMES).

24. Monitor and reinforce memory-enhancing exercises (e.g., crosswords) and memory loss coping strategies. Adapt exercises to fit the patient's changing needs. Stop the tasks that produce frustration, loss of self-esteem, or guilt.

25. Develop a plan for cognitively and socially stimulating (but not overwhelming) activities.

26. Assist the patient in coming to an understanding and acceptance of the current limitations and a possible future course.

27. Evaluate the patient's need for a greater level of supervision (due to being a danger to himself/herself or

unable to care for his/her own basic needs) and with the patient, family, and other care team members, arrange for appropriate level of assisted living.

__. _____
    _____
__. _____
    _____
__. _____
    _____

DIAGNOSTIC SUGGESTIONS

Axis I:	293.0	Delirium Due to (Axis III Disorder)
	291.0	Alcohol Intoxication or Withdrawal Delirium
	292.0	Sedative, Hypnotic, or Anxiolytic Withdrawal
	292.81	Other or Unknown Substance-Induced Delirium
	290.xx	Dementia of the Alzheimer's Type or Vascular Dementia
	294.1	Dementia Due to (Head Trauma, Parkinson's Disease, Huntington's Disease, or Axis III Disorder)
	290.10	Dementia Due to Pick's Disease or Creutzfeldt-Jakob Disease
	294.8	Dementia NOS
	291.2	Alcohol-Induced Persisting Dementia
	294.0	Amnestic Disorder Due to (Axis III Disorder)
	291.1	Alcohol-Induced Persisting Amnestic Disorder
	294.8	Amnestic Disorder NOS
	294.9	Cognitive Disorder NOS
	995.2	Adverse Effects of Medication NOS
	780.9	Age-Related Cognitive Decline

NUTRITIONAL DEFICITS UNRESOLVED

BEHAVIORAL DEFINITIONS

1. Significant weight loss that is becoming life-threatening.
2. Unwillingness to eat food that is prepared and presented.
3. Conflict with the family/caregivers about food and eating.
4. Inability or unwillingness to prepare nourishing meals.
5. Inability or unwillingness of caregivers to prepare nourishing meals.
6. Statements about food that suggest hopelessness or depression (e.g., food "doesn't taste good," "doesn't matter," "isn't worth the trouble," or "Why bother eating?").
7. Statements about food that suggest paranoia (e.g., "This food is poisoned.").
8. Caregiver reports distress regarding the patient's declining nutritional status.

—. _____
_____

—. _____
_____

—. _____
_____

LONG-TERM GOALS

1. Take emergency measures consistent with advance directives to protect the patient from life-threatening malnutrition.
2. Identify and implement a care plan to provide ongoing support for adequate nutrition and hydration consistent with advance directives.

3. Identify cause(s) of nutritional deficits.
4. Resolve depression, anxiety, and/or paranoia that may be interfering with the desire to eat.
5. Resolve social and interpersonal issues that may be interfering with eating.
6. Resolve medical/physical issues that may be interfering with nutrition.

—. _____

_____

—. _____

_____

—. _____

_____

SHORT-TERM OBJECTIVES

1. Consent to participate in an evaluation of nutritional deficits if decisionally capable; surrogate consents if the patient is not decisionally capable. (1)

2. Patient, staff, and/or family describe the nutritional problem in specific detail, giving perspectives on causes and possible solutions. (2, 3, 27, 28, 29)

3. Review advance directives regarding nutrition and hydration if such directives have already been signed. (4, 5, 6)

4. Cooperate with an evaluation of decision-making capacity. (7, 9)

5. Sign advance directives, including nutrition/hydration issues, if decisionally

THERAPEUTIC INTERVENTIONS

1. Obtain consent from the patient or surrogate to address the problem of nutritional deficit, including consent to discuss issues with others involved.

2. Ask the patient, staff, and family to explain as completely as possible their perspective on the nutritional problem (e.g., Is the problem the ability or the willingness to eat? Does it seem to be associated with an illness, a medication, an event? What emotions does the patient express about food and eating? How do others react? What solutions have been tried?).

3. Obtain an accurate current weight for the patient and compare with history data.

capable and directives are not already completed. (8, 27, 28, 29)

6. Cooperate with emergency measures to improve nutritional status consistent with advance directives. (10, 26, 27, 28, 29)

7. Verbalize preferences about food and fluid intake. (11, 27, 28)

8. Patient, staff, and/or family keep a daily record of the patient's verbal and nonverbal reactions to foods and fluids. (12)

9. Cooperate with a psychological evaluation to determine if depression, anxiety, paranoia, or other mental illness is interfering with either nutritional intake or decision-making capacity. (13)

10. Complete treatment for psychological conditions. (14)

11. Cooperate with a medical evaluation to determine if illness, medication, throat spasms, mouth or throat pain are associated with nutritional deficits. (15)

12. Cooperate with a dental evaluation to determine if poor dentition is associated with nutritional deficits. (16)

13. Comply with a medical/dental recommendations for treatment. (17)

14. Cooperate with a swallowing evaluation to determine the presence of coughing,

4. Instruct the patient/family to bring a copy of advance directives to a conjoint session.

5. If the patient is able, encourage him/her to read and explain all existing advance directives. If unable, ask the surrogate to do so, assisting as necessary. Draw attention to any reference to nutrition/hydration (usually specified as "do/do not administer artificial nutrition/hydration").

6. Lead the discussion until all present are comfortable with the meaning and implications of the advance directives in the current situation. Encourage the patient and the family to get a detailed explanation of nutrition/hydration options (including feeding tubes) from the physician.

7. If advance directives have not been completed, evaluate the patient's capacity to execute them. (See the Decisional Incapacity Unresolved chapter in this *Planner.*)

8. If the patient is decisionally capable, instruct him/her to execute advance directives with the help of a private or publicly funded eldercare lawyer.

9. If the patient is not decisionally capable, help the family/caregivers/physician

choking, or aspiration during eating or drinking. (18)

15. Comply with the recommendations regarding food and
fluid consistency to compensate for a swallowing dysfunction. (19)

16. Cooperate with a dietary or
nutritional evaluation to
determine daily food and
fluid nutrition, calorie, and
volume intakes, and bowel
and bladder output. (20)

17. Comply with the dietary
recommendations regarding
diet modifications, dietary
supplements, food preparation and presentation, timing of meals, and so forth.
(21)

18. Cooperate with an evaluation of environmental and
psychosocial factors that
may negatively impact
nutritional status. (22)

19. Comply with environmental
and social recommenda-
tions. (23, 24)

20. Identify weight and nutritional goals, the plan of
care, and the persons who
will monitor and follow up
on progress. (25)

21. Identify an alternate plan
and responsible persons if
nutritional status decom-
pensates. (26)

22. Maintain maximum autonomy by direct expression of
feelings and preferences
regarding nutrition and
hydration. (27, 28, 29)

determine which individual
will be the surrogate
decision-maker.

10. Refer to the physician for
emergency treatment of life-
threatening malnutrition or
dehydration as consistent
with advance directives
regarding feeding tubes, IV
fluids, and/or hospitalization.

11. Encourage the patient to
verbalize preferences about
foods and fluids (e.g., what
types, flavors, consistency,
sweet/salty/sour/spicy, time
of day, physical and social
environment, etc.).

12. Instruct the patient or fam-
ily/caregiver to keep a daily
record of the patient's food
and fluid intake, specifying
the patient's verbal and
nonverbal reactions to
everything that was taken
in or offered.

13. Conduct or refer for a psychological evaluation to
assess the possible contributions—depression, anxiety,
paranoia, or other mental
illness—to nutritional
deficits or ability to make
decisions about nutrition/
hydration.

14. Treat depression, anxiety,
paranoia, or other condi-
tions. (See the Depression,
Anxiety, and Paranoid
Ideation chapters in this
Planner.)

15. Refer to a physician for an
evaluation of medical condi-

—. _____

_____

—. _____

_____

—. _____

_____

tions (e.g., oral cancer, oral abscess), medications, or throat spasms that could be interfering with adequate nutritional intake.

16. Refer to a dentist for an evaluation of oral pain, bleeding gums, or a poorly fitting denture/bridge that could be interfering with adequate nutritional intake.

17. Discuss a medical/dental care plan with the physician/dentist; encourage patient compliance with the plan; monitor compliance and discuss with the patient, family, and treating professionals as appropriate.

18. Refer to a speech therapist/nutritionist/physician for an evaluation of swallowing function and recommendations for modification of diet to accommodate problems with swallowing (dysphagia).

19. Discuss a dietary care plan with the speech therapist/nutritionist; encourage patient compliance with the dietary plan; monitor compliance and discuss with the patient and treating professionals as appropriate.

20. Refer to a dietitian/nutritionist for an evaluation of daily food and fluid nutrition, calorie, and volume intakes, and bowel and bladder output.

21. Discuss with the dietitian/ nutritionist recommendations regarding diet modifications (e.g., more nutritional foods), dietary supplements (e.g., Ensure), food preparation and presentation (e.g., adding more appealing flavors and textures), and meal timing (smaller, more frequent meals). Encourage and monitor patient compliance with dietary plan.

22. Conduct or refer for an evaluation of the environmental and psychosocial factors (e.g., inadequate kitchen equipment, caregiver knowledge of and motivation to meet the patient's nutritional preferences, caregiver compliance with special nutritional needs, sufficient income to buy food, and need for/availability of home-delivered meals) that may be interfering with adequate nutrition.

23. Conduct conjoint sessions with the patient and caregiver(s) to review the need for adequate nutrition, and the environmental and psychosocial barriers to adequate nutrition. Develop a plan to overcome the barriers and designate a responsible person to follow up (e.g., contact the Area Agency on Aging to arrange for home-delivered meals).

24. Monitor compliance with the environmental and psychosocial care plans, and adjust the plan as necessary.

25. Integrate the findings from all consulting professionals into a single plan of care, specifying weight and nutritional goals, steps to achieve goals, and the responsible party to accomplish, monitor, and follow up on each step; distribute an integrated plan to all involved parties.

26. Through joint meetings or by telephone, help all involved parties develop an alternate, more intensive plan, and identify the responsible persons should nutritional status decline.

27. Encourage the patient to continually explore and directly express (to the therapist, physician, and family) feelings and preferences regarding nutrition/hydration.

28. Continually remind all involved parties that issues involving food and water (nutrition/hydration) are very emotionally laden, and all individuals need to be aware of, and separate, their own emotional reactions from the objective facts of the specific situation.

29. Ask that all involved parties refrain from unneces-

sary use of emotionally charged phrases such as "starve to death" or "die of thirst."

—. _____
_____

—. _____
_____

—. _____
_____

DIAGNOSTIC SUGGESTIONS

Axis I:	296.xx	Major Depressive Disorder
	300.4	Dysthymic Disorder
	311	Depressive Disorder NOS
	300.02	Generalized Anxiety Disorder
	300.00	Anxiety Disorder NOS
	309.xx	Adjustment Disorder
	297.1	Delusional Disorder
	290.20	Dementia of the Alzheimer's Type, with Delusions
	290.42	Vascular Dementia with Delusions
	310.1	Personality Change Due to (Axis III Disorder)
	316	Psychological Factors Affecting Medical Condition
	995.2	Adverse Effects of Medication NOS
	_____	_____
	_____	_____

OBSESSIVE-COMPULSIVE DISORDER (OCD)

BEHAVIORAL DEFINITIONS

1. Recurrent and persistent thoughts, impulses, or images that are intrusive, senseless, and time-consuming.
2. Failed attempts to ignore or control these thoughts or impulses or neutralize them with other thoughts and actions.
3. Recognition that obsessive thoughts are a product of own mind.
4. Repetitive behaviors or mental acts that are done in response to obsessive thoughts or rigid rules.
5. Repetitive behavior that is done to neutralize or prevent distress; however, the behavior is not realistically connected with what it is designed to prevent, or is excessive.
6. Thoughts or behaviors cause significant anxiety or distress, interfere with daily routine or functioning, and/or disrupt social activities or relationships.
7. Recognition that thoughts and/or behaviors are excessive or unreasonable.

—. _____
   _____
—. _____
   _____
—. _____
   _____

LONG-TERM GOALS

1. Reduce time involved with or interference from obsessions and compulsions.

2. Reduce or resolve stressful situations that fuel obsessive-compulsive behavior patterns.
3. Improve functioning in daily routines, social activities, and relationships.
4. Learn stress management skills to prevent obsessive-compulsive response.
5. Learn problem-solving skills to resolve stressful situations.
6. Manage environmental stressors in a way to reduce psychological pressure.
7. Accept help as necessary from formal and informal support systems to reduce stress.

___. _____
_____
___. _____
_____
___. _____
_____

SHORT-TERM OBJECTIVES

THERAPEUTIC INTERVENTIONS

1. Identify the specific thoughts or behaviors that are most disturbing or most contribute to impaired functioning. (1, 2)

2. Verbalize an understanding of the role of obsessive thoughts in producing anxiety and compulsive behaviors in controlling anxiety. (3, 4)

3. Consent to participate in the treatment of the disorder. (5, 6, 7)

4. Keep a daily journal to establish frequency, intensity, time of day, duration, and situations, people, thoughts, moods, and behav-

1. Ask the patient to verbalize or list specific obsessive thoughts or compulsive behaviors in detail, and rank-order the symptoms on the basis of how disturbing they are.

2. Help the patient to identify whether and/or how each symptom interferes with daily functioning and/or relationships.

3. Teach the patient how the obsessions cause anxiety and distress, but are coming from within his/her mind, and are therefore under the his/her control.

iors that precede or follow the OCD symptoms. (8)

5. Compile a list of all medical conditions, approximate date of diagnosis, and the treating physician(s). (9)

6. Compile a list of all prescribed and over-the-counter medications, dosage, and time of day they are taken. (10)

7. Accept referral to a gero-psychiatrist to evaluate obsessive-compulsive symptoms, illnesses, and medications and treat as appropriate. (11, 12)

8. Comply with physician-ordered treatments and/or changes in medications. (13, 14, 15)

9. Identify and clarify the patterns to symptom precipitants and consequences. (8, 16, 17)

10. List the negative consequences of obsessive thoughts. (18)

11. Use thought stopping and thought challenging to reduce obsessive thoughts. (19, 20)

12. Practice and implement relaxation techniques to reduce stress and anxiety. (21, 22, 23)

13. Identify daily routine activities that have been effective at reducing stress and anxiety in the past. (24)

14. Make lifestyle changes in diet, exercise, and pleasur-

4. Teach the patient how the compulsive behaviors are performed to decrease anxiety, but in fact serve to disrupt daily life and interfere with more satisfying activities.

5. Explain to the patient that this disorder is highly treatable, usually with a combination of behavioral psychotherapy and pharmacotherapy.

6. Discuss with the patient the course of treatment: rule out medical causes; establish the baseline; evaluate for pharmacotherapy; learn and practice behavioral interventions.

7. Obtain consent to address the obsessive-compulsive disorder, including consent to discuss issues with other involved parties, such as physicians, staff, and family, as necessary.

8. Assign the patient to record OCD symptom occurrence, time of day, intensity (1 to 10), duration, and situations, people, thoughts, moods, and behaviors that accompany the symptoms.

9. Assign the patient to produce a list of all medical conditions, approximate date of diagnosis, and the treating physician(s).

10. Assign the patient to produce a list of all prescribed and over-the-counter medications, dosage, and time of

able habits that will reduce stress and anxiety. (25, 26)

15. Participate in, learn, and practice behavioral control methods to reduce compulsive behaviors. (27, 28, 29)

16. Adjust the living situation (e.g., move from housing that is too demanding to a more supportive environment) to reduce stress. (30, 31, 32)

17. Evaluate realistically the need for additional support in performing Activities of Daily Living, and develop a plan to obtain such support to reduce stress. (33, 34, 35)

18. Demonstrate an increase in assertiveness skills. (36)

19. Use assertiveness to deal constructively with situations that need to be confronted to reduce stress. (36, 37)

20. Accept a referral to a specialty clinic for obsessive-compulsive disorder if the symptoms persist. (38, 39)

—. _____
  _____

—. _____
  _____

—. _____
  _____

day they are taken. If the patient is unable to complete this task, ask that all medication containers be brought to the next session.

11. Collect, organize, and analyze data on obsessive-compulsive symptoms, medical conditions, and medications.

12. Refer to a geropsychiatrist for an evaluation, and keep the primary care physician informed of issues and progress.

13. Obtain from the geropsychiatrist the ordered treatments/changes in medications to reinforce the patient's compliance with changes.

14. Review physician-ordered treatments/changes with the patient (and if appropriate, the family or staff).

15. Ensure that new medications, dosages, and administration schedules are written down in checklist form to facilitate compliance.

16. Help the patient to recognize patterns associated with symptoms by sorting out and identifying precipitants from the consequences.

17. Help the patient identify the most intense or frequent precipitants, and identify the consequences that help to perpetuate the symptoms.

18. Assist the patient in identifying negative consequences of obsessive thoughts (e.g., anxiety and distress, feeling driven to compulsive behaviors, and inability to concentrate).

19. Teach the patient to pair an obsessive thought with an abrupt, aversive stimulus, such as the silent shout "STOP!", visualizing a stop sign in his/her mind, or the pop of a rubber band on the wrist.

20. Teach the patient to challenge an obsessive thought with a rational thought, such as replacing "I think I left the stove on," with "I've never left the stove on."

21. Teach the patient relaxation techniques, beginning with deep breathing, and proceeding to progressive muscle relaxation if he/she is able.

22. Teach the patient positive imagery techniques with muscle relaxation if he/she is able to use imagery.

23. Provide the patient with a personalized audiotape and suggest the purchase of a relaxation videotape if he/she owns a VCR.

24. Assist the patient in identifying the most effective personal stress management techniques from his/her past experience (e.g., praying, walking, baking, telephoning a friend), and

encourage daily scheduling of these activities.

25. Review the presence of healthy lifestyle practices with the patient (i.e., diet, exercise, caffeine and nicotine consumption, pleasurable activities, etc.).

26. Help the patient develop a plan to reduce or eliminate stress- and anxiety-producers and improve wellness.

27. Design and implement a program of in vivo or imagined stimulus exposure and response prevention to the trigger stimuli.

28. Design and implement a program of reinforcement of responses that are incompatible with compulsive behaviors.

29. Teach and encourage family and staff participation in support of a behavioral treatment program as appropriate.

30. Teach the patient the concept of matching an individual's capacities and environmental demands, so that the individual doesn't become overwhelmed.

31. Help the patient determine if the current living situation is appropriate to his/her capacity, or if a change is warranted given current or anticipated capacity.

32. Assist the patient with the psychological components of

making a change in the living situation (e.g., thinking
about alternatives, choosing, planning, anticipating
and grieving losses, adapting, etc.).

33. Assess if additional help is
needed to accomplish the
Activities of Daily Living or
the Instrumental Activities
of Daily Living.

34. Refer the patient to aging
services to obtain additional
supports, such as the Area
Agency on Aging, faith-
based aging services, private
geriatric care management,
or other community services
as available.

35. Discuss the patient's willingness to involve an informal support network (e.g.,
family members, neighbors,
religious counselors) in providing additional care and
services; develop a plan to
ask for help.

36. Use role-playing, modeling,
and behavioral rehearsal
to train the patient in
assertiveness or refer to
an assertiveness training
class.

37. Encourage the patient to
resolve situations that can
be assertively changed to
alleviate stress (e.g., discussing conflict openly, stating personal wishes in "I"
statements, etc.).

38. Consult with the attending
geropsychiatrist regarding
pharmacotherapy changes

if symptoms are persisting at a significant level.

39. Refer the patient to a specialty clinic for obsessive-compulsive disorder if the symptoms persist at a level that significantly interferes with function or well-being.

__. _____
_____

__. _____
_____

__. _____
_____

DIAGNOSTIC SUGGESTIONS

Axis I:	300.3	Obsessive-Compulsive Disorder
	300.00	Anxiety Disorder NOS
	296.xx	Major Depressive Disorder
	303.90	Alcohol Dependence
	304.10	Sedative, Hypnotic, or Anxiolytic Dependence
	_____	_____
	_____	_____

PARANOID IDEATION

BEHAVIORAL DEFINITIONS

1. Statements of erroneous beliefs involving a misinterpretation of perceptions or experiences.
2. Statements that one is being persecuted: tormented, stolen from, poisoned, spied on, and so forth.
3. Erroneous statements that general environmental cues are directed at self: that casual gestures, comments, and/or laughing of others are all directed at oneself.
4. Complaints that people are talking about self in the absence of any conversation.
5. Refusal to allow home health, meal delivery, or repair services in the house because of irrational fear of harm to self.
6. Activity taken to protect oneself from harm in the absence of actual threat (e.g., barricading doors, refusing to answer the phone, storing weapons, making threatening phone calls to others, refusing to eat "poisoned" food, etc.).
7. Withdrawal from social interaction and refusal to participate in activity programs due to verbalized irrational suspicions.
8. Overt signs of inexplicable hostility and extreme irritability toward others.
9. Unexplained measures that break off ties with relatives, such as refusing phone calls, visits, removing them as estate beneficiaries, and so forth.

—. _____
   _____

—. _____
   _____

—. _____
   _____

LONG-TERM GOALS

1. Terminate danger to self or others.
2. Develop trust in at least one other person.
3. Reduce or eliminate erroneous irrational suspicious beliefs.
4. Reduce or eliminate hostility and irritability exhibited toward others.
5. Reduce or eliminate feelings of fear and insecurity.
6. Cooperate with necessary and desirable medical, social, and home services.
7. Participate in, and enjoy the benefits of, a social support system.
8. Interact with family members in a mutually satisfying way.

—. _____
_____
—. _____
_____
—. _____
_____

SHORT-TERM OBJECTIVES

1. Consent to participate in a psychiatric evaluation if decisionally capable; surrogate consents if the patient is not decisionally capable. (1)

2. Cooperate with necessary safety precautions to protect self and others from harm. (2)

3. Tolerate brief daily non-threatening contacts from the therapist. (3)

4. Tolerate a 20-minute non-threatening session with the therapist. (4)

THERAPEUTIC INTERVENTIONS

1. Obtain consent from the patient or surrogate to address the problem of paranoid ideation, including consent to discuss issues with other involved parties (e.g., family, staff, physician).

2. Evaluate or refer to a physician for an evaluation of the severity of danger to self and others; take the necessary immediate safety precautions (e.g., removal of weapons or barricades, temporary termination of telephone service, removal from current environment, hospitalization, etc.).

5. Tolerate a 30-minute non-threatening session with the therapist. (5)

6. Verbalize personal concerns to the therapist as a manifestation of trust. (6, 7)

7. Give permission to the therapist to arrange for an interdisciplinary evaluation. (8, 9)

8. Converse with the therapist to reduce anxiety if it rises to the point of interfering with evaluations. (9)

9. Cooperate with a medical evaluation to identify the possible organic causative factors to the paranoid ideation. (10)

10. Comply with a hearing evaluation. (11)

11. Participate in a vision evaluation. (12)

12. Cooperate with a psychological assessment. (13)

13. Comply with a neuropsychological evaluation. (14)

14. Complete treatment for confounding or coexisting medical/psychiatric conditions, adverse drug reactions, and/or sensory impairment. (15)

15. Take psychotropic medications as prescribed by the physician and report as to the effectiveness and side effects. (16, 17)

16. Cooperate with social or elder services to help with the arrangements for appro-

3. Drop by (if residential) or telephone the patient every day for a 2- to 5-minute contact, allowing him/her to determine the content of the conversation or activity.

4. Gradually increase contact time to 20 minutes face-to-face, still allowing the patient to determine the content of the conversation or activity.

5. Increase contact time to 30 minutes face-to-face, with the patient determining the content of the conversation or activity.

6. Gently begin introducing topics that seem to be anxiety-producing for the patient, as tolerated.

7. Reduce the patient's anxiety with a reassuring, calm, gentle, rational manner, providing practical help, problem-solving, and advocacy.

8. Encourage the patient to participate in an interdisciplinary evaluation, offering to provide reassurance throughout.

9. Contract with the patient that rather than refusing or leaving the evaluations, the patient will contact the therapist for reassurance and help.

10. Refer to a physician for an evaluation of medical conditions and medications (prescribed and OTC) that could

priate residential placement or in-home services. (15, 18)

17. Verbalize rational explanations for others' behaviors in place of the irrational belief that they represent attempts to harm or humiliate the patient. (19, 20)

18. Describe clearly the limits of tolerance for emotional and physical proximity to others. (21)

19. Verbalize recognition that tolerance for others may need to be adjusted to facilitate health and well-being. (22)

20. Verbalize a willingness to be in physical proximity to others who were formerly deemed too threatening to be near (neighbors, family members, service providers, roommates). (23, 24)

21. Demonstrate socially appropriate (even if guarded) behavior when others initiate friendly contact. (25, 26, 27)

22. List social activities that are enjoyable but not experienced as intrusive or too emotionally demanding. (28)

23. Attend one activity or event per day in the presence of others, without fear or hostility. (29, 30, 31)

24. Identify one family member or (potential) friend with whom a trusting relationship could be built/restored. (32, 33, 34, 35)

be causing paranoid ideation, or psychotropic medications that could help control the symptoms.

11. Refer to a hearing specialist for an evaluation of the impairment that could be causing or contributing to paranoid ideation.

12. Refer the patient for an eye exam.

13. Conduct or refer for a psychological evaluation to determine the psychiatric and functional history, onset of problem, precipitants, and psychosocial stressors (e.g., being overwhelmed by demands of current living situation; feeling powerless to escape a difficult roommate or neighbor) that could be causing or contributing to paranoid ideation.

14. Conduct or refer for a neuropsychological evaluation to determine if cognitive status could be causing or contributing to paranoid ideation.

15. Discuss the results of the evaluations with the patient, family, physician/ psychiatrist, and staff as appropriate; develop a plan to address treatable medical/psychiatric, sensory, psychosocial, and psychological causes for the paranoid ideation.

16. Physician prescribes and titrates psychotropic medications.

25. Use creative arts projects, music listening, or journaling to identify and express feelings of anxiety, fear, and alienation; discuss and work through the feelings with the therapist. (36, 37)

26. Staff and family caregivers understand the anxiety and fear underlying the irrational beliefs and behavior. (38)

27. Caregivers maintain moderate physical distance that is respectful of the patient's privacy, while maintaining a calm and friendly demeanor. (39, 40, 41)

28. Reduce or eliminate hostile exchanges with the family, caregivers, and others in the environment. (42, 43, 44)

29. Identify the rising feelings of anxiety and fear. (45)

30. Develop/agree to a plan to get an objective opinion and reassurance from a family member, friend, or therapist if feelings of anxiety and fear become uncomfortable. (46)

—. _____
   _____

—. _____
   _____

—. _____
   _____

17. Staff/family/self administers medications and monitors for side effects and effectiveness.

18. Refer to social or elder services to help the patient and family with relocation or initiation of in-home services if the current living situation is too demanding for patient's cognitive, physical, or psychiatric status.

19. Gently offer alternative explanations for others' behavior, without getting into a debate.

20. Offer more realistic appraisals of others, calmly suggesting that the probability of harm from others is low.

21. Encourage the patient to verbalize personal boundaries for emotional and physical proximity, respecting historical personality patterns.

22. Help the patient distinguish the point at which a low tolerance for interaction could interfere with health and well-being.

23. Help the patient problem-solve how to interact with others to obtain necessary goods, services, or support while maintaining feelings of personal safety.

24. Help the patient develop a systematic desensitization process for increasing physical proximity while main-

taining feelings of personal safety (e.g., meal delivery person can leave meals on the front porch for one week; then hand the meals through a partially opened door for one week; then give them to the patient in the foyer for one week; and finally, put them in the freezer, etc.).

25. Observe the patient in a social situation (in residence, conjoint session, or group therapy).

26. Teach the patient the importance—if only as a formality or instrumental necessity—of maintaining cordial relationships with caregivers and others.

27. Develop role-play scenarios that are part of the patient's everyday life and practice basic, if minimal, appropriate social responses to friendly contact.

28. Review social activities that are available to the patient, in residence or community, where he/she could be in a nondemanding, nonemotionally threatening social situation: concerts, plays, lectures, and other noninteractive events.

29. Teach the patient the importance of intellectual stimulation and the positive effects of being out in the world.

30. Reassure the patient of the possibility of gaining the

benefits of intellectual and social stimulation without becoming overstimulated or emotionally threatened (by choosing noninteractive events).

31. Slowly begin a program of the patient's attendance at social events, providing reassurance and reinforcement as necessary; work up to one activity or event per day in the presence of others.

32. Review the patient's history of social interactions with family, friends, neighbors, roommates, and so forth.

33. Teach the patient the benefits of having at least one other person (beyond the therapist) whom he/she can trust.

34. Assign the patient to select an individual with whom to develop or restore a trusting relationship.

35. Encourage and reinforce the patient for initiating friendly contact with the targeted individual; support the patient in the development of the relationship, including conjoint sessions if necessary.

36. Identify a medium through which the patient can comfortably identify, experience, and express feelings.

37. Instruct the patient how to use creative arts or indirect verbal media (such as jour-

naling) to learn to identify and cope with his/her troubling feelings and thoughts.

38. Instruct the staff and family caregivers in the mental illness, and explain how hostile, angry, or bizarre behaviors are usually in response to a perceived threat that produces significant fear and anxiety.

39. Discuss with the staff and family caregivers the primary sources of fear and anxiety for the patient; problem-solve how to interact with the patient in a way that reduces fear, including maintenance of a calm and friendly demeanor.

40. Teach the staff/family caregivers the importance of physical and psychological distance, and the need for respect, privacy, and dignity.

41. Help the staff/family caregivers achieve personal distance by understanding that the hostility and anger are not directed to them as persons, but that "it's the mental illness talking."

42. In conjoint sessions, negotiate the rights of both the patient and the staff/family caregivers to be treated with respect and dignity.

43. Achieve agreement between the patient and the caregivers on fundamentals of cordial social interactions; set limits on the expression of hostility.

44. Contract with the patient and the caregivers to give calm and nonaccusatory feedback about the appropriateness of the social interactions of the other.

45. Assist the patient in using either verbally direct or indirect (arts, journal) means to be able to identify a rise in anxiety or fear.

46. Help the patient develop a written plan to use when his/her anxiety and fear increase to the point of discomfort, that includes checking perceptions with a trusted friend/family member or the therapist, and identifying stressors that could be causing the increase in distress.

—. _____

_____

—. _____

_____

—. _____

_____

DIAGNOSTIC SUGGESTIONS

Axis I:	290.20	Dementia of the Alzheimer's Type, with Delusions
	290.42	Vascular Dementia, with Delusions
	300.23	Social Phobia
	310.1	Personality Change Due to (Axis III Disorder)
	295.30	Schizophrenia, Paranoid Type
	297.1	Delusional Disorder
	995.2	Adverse Effects of Medication NOS
	_____	_____
	_____	_____

PHOBIA/PANIC/AGORAPHOBIA

BEHAVIORAL DEFINITIONS

1. Intense fear of being in a place or situation perceived as dangerous and from which escape may be difficult or embarrassing.
2. Intense fear of being in the presence of a specific object, resulting in significant distress or avoidance to the point of interfering with daily living.
3. Intense fear of social situations in which embarrassment may occur, resulting in significant distress or avoidance to the point of interfering with daily living.
4. Rapid onset of somatic symptoms (nausea/diarrhea, sweating, trembling, heart palpitations, chest pain, shortness of breath, choking, numbness, chills/hot flashes, or dizziness) or cognitive symptoms (depersonalization or derealization, fear of losing control, fear of dying) associated with intense anxiety.
5. Resistance to leaving home in spite of reassurance by the physician that it is acceptable/advisable to do so, especially when disabled, incontinent, or on oxygen.
6. Anticipation that a mild physical symptom or medication side effect will have a catastrophic outcome.

—. _____
_____
—. _____
_____
—. _____
_____

LONG-TERM GOALS

1. Able to be in the presence of the previously feared object or situation without debilitating anxiety and need to escape.
2. Terminate or significantly reduce the intensity and frequency of panic attack symptoms leading to normal participation in daily routines.
3. Can independently and freely leave home and comfortably be in social environments.
4. Eliminate or reduce unnecessary use of medical services due to excessive and unreasonable fear of perceived life-threatening symptoms.
5. Improve the ability to realistically evaluate the danger associated with objects, people, and situations.
6. Improve the ability to correctly categorize and act upon somatic symptoms.

—. _____

_____

—. _____

_____

—. _____

_____

SHORT-TERM OBJECTIVES

1. Identify the fear and describe the specific somatic and/or cognitive symptoms that occur in the feared situation. (1, 2)

2. Verbalize an understanding of the general physical and cognitive manifestations of and possible causes for phobia/panic/agoraphobia. (3, 4, 5)

3. Keep a daily journal of symptoms to record the

THERAPEUTIC INTERVENTIONS

1. Assign the patient to verbalize or list all symptoms that are experienced in feared situations.

2. Help the patient to identify whether and/or how each symptom interferes with daily functioning and/or relationships.

3. Teach the patient to differentiate the specific symptoms that may be experienced in feared situations, especially the distinc-

details of their occurrence. (6, 7)

4. Compile a list of all prescribed and over-the-counter medications, dosage, and time of day they are taken. (8)

5. Compile a list of all medical conditions, approximate date of diagnosis, and the treating physician(s). (9)

6. Give written consent for the physician(s) and/or designated family members to be contacted if necessary. (10, 11)

7. Accept a referral to a physician to review possible relationships between somatic and cognitive symptoms, illnesses, and medications. (12, 13, 14)

8. Comply with the physician-ordered changes in medications, dosages, or administration schedules to alleviate somatic and/or cognitive symptoms. (15, 16, 17, 22)

9. Accept a referral to a geropsychiatrist for evaluation of symptoms, illnesses, and medications and treatment as appropriate. (13, 18)

10. Comply with geropsychiatrist-ordered treatments and/or changes in medications. (19, 20, 21, 22)

11. Identify and clarify the patterns to symptom precipitants and consequences. (6, 7, 23, 24)

tion between cognitive and somatic symptoms.

4. Assist the patient in identifying his/her personal discrete symptoms.

5. Discuss with the patient the possible etiologies of these symptoms: illnesses (such as endocrine, cardiovascular, respiratory, metabolic, and neurological conditions), prescribed and over-the-counter medications, and maladaptive learned responses to stressors.

6. Develop a simple chart for the patient to record the time, duration, and intensity (rated 1 to 10) of symptoms, and to record the precipitating and consequent situations, events, people, thoughts, moods, and behaviors that are associated with symptoms.

7. Assign the patient to complete a symptom chart on a daily basis.

8. Assign the patient to produce a list of all prescribed and over-the-counter medications, dosage, and time of day they are taken. If patient is unable to complete this task, ask that all medication containers be brought to the next session for review.

9. Assign the patient to produce a list of all medical conditions, approximate date of diagnosis, and the treating physician(s).

12. Verbalize how the short-term anxiety reduction associated with escape or avoidance behaviors eventually leads to negative life consequences. (25)

13. List the apparent reinforcements of phobia/panic/agoraphobia, such as reducing distress by avoidance of stressful situations. (26)

14. Make a commitment to learn constructive ways to cope with feared situations and achieve positive goals. (27, 28, 29)

15. Verbalize an understanding of cognitive and behavioral control methods to reduce panic response. (30, 31)

16. Allow exposure to paniclike somatic symptoms in a controlled, gradual way. (31)

17. Identify distorted, negative self-talk that mediates intensification of anxiety symptoms. (32)

18. Verbalize and implement positive, realistic, anxiety-reducing self-talk. (33)

19. Practice and implement controlled, deep breathing as a means of alleviating panic symptoms. (34)

20. Learn, practice, and implement relaxation techniques. (35, 36)

21. Create a hierarchy of feared situations that are the basis for the phobic response. (37, 38)

10. Discuss with the patient the necessity for working with his/her primary care physician to determine if there may be a physical etiology to the anxiety symptoms. Obtain written consent from the patient to speak with the physician.

11. Discuss with the patient the need or desire to involve designated family members in treatment. If the patient is unable to produce accurate medical information, or reports family involvement in symptom control, obtain written permission to contact the family members.

12. Collect, organize, and analyze data on anxiety symptoms, medical conditions, and medications. If medical etiology seems possible, refer to the primary care physician for a medical evaluation.

13. Explain to the patient's primary care physician that psychotherapeutic treatment without medication would be tried first, but if symptoms are severe or persistent, a referral to a geropsychiatrist would be necessary.

14. Keep the primary care physician informed of the patient's progress in reducing anxiety symptoms, and the desirability of avoiding the use of anxiolytics if possible.

22. Use the in vivo exposure technique coupled with cognitive and behavioral coping skills to reduce the anxiety response to the feared object or situation. (33, 34, 35, 39)

23. Use systematic desensitization to imagined feared stimuli coupled with relaxation and deep breathing to reduce the anxiety response to the feared object or situation. (34, 35, 40)

24. Identify daily routine activities that have been effective at reducing stress and anxiety symptoms in the past. (41)

25. Make lifestyle changes in diet, exercise, and pleasurable habits that will reduce stress and anxiety. (42)

26. Cooperate with a substance abuse evaluation to determine the extent of chemical dependence. (43)

27. Eliminate reliance on substances on which a dependence has developed and that have been abused to control anxiety symptoms. (44)

28. Adjust the living situation (e.g., move from housing that is too demanding to more supportive environment) to reduce stress. (45, 46, 47)

29. Evaluate realistically the need for additional support in performing Activities of

15. Obtain from the physician the ordered changes in medication, dosages, or administration schedules to reinforce the patient's compliance with the changes.

16. Review physician-ordered changes with the patient and, if involved, a family member or staff.

17. Ensure that new medications, dosages, and administration schedules are written down in checklist form to facilitate compliance.

18. Refer to a geropsychiatrist for the evaluation and development of a joint plan of care.

19. Obtain from the geropsychiatrist the treatment plan to reinforce the patient's compliance.

20. Review psychiatrist-ordered treatments/changes with the patient (and if appropriate, family or staff).

21. Ensure that medications, dosages, and administration schedules are written down in checklist form to facilitate compliance.

22. Keep both the patient's primary care physician and geropsychiatrist informed of issues and progress.

23. Help the patient to recognize patterns associated with symptoms by sorting out and identifying precipitants from consequences.

Daily Life and develop a plan to obtain such support to reduce stress. (48, 49, 50)

30. Use assertiveness to deal constructively with situations that need to be confronted to reduce stress. (51)

31. Accept referral to specialty clinic for anxiety disorders. (52)

—. _____

  _____

—. _____

  _____

—. _____

  _____

24. Help the patient identify the most intense or frequent precipitants, and identify the consequences that help to reinforce or perpetuate symptoms.

25. Assign the patient to verbalize negative consequences of symptoms, such as mental and physical distress, social dysfunction, impaired performance of work and daily activities.

26. Assist the patient in identifying how the current pattern is maintained by reducing anxiety symptoms through avoidance.

27. Instill hope in the patient by explaining that these disorders are highly treatable with specific techniques, with excellent success rates.

28. Teach the patient that these disorders usually occur in patients with a biological predisposition to experience anxiety, who then learned inappropriate cognitions and behaviors to control the anxiety.

29. Teach the patient that what has been learned can be unlearned, and that will be the focus of treatment; with help from the primary care physician, teach the patient to differentiate anxiety symptoms from medical symptoms.

30. Explain the use of cognitive and behavioral techniques to control anxiety (e.g., see

the Panic Control Treatment (PCT) described in *Mastery of Your Anxiety and Panic,* by Barlow and Craske, 1994).

31. Provide the patient with systemized exposure to paniclike sensations using PCT techniques.

32. Assist the patient in identifying the distorted, negative automatic thoughts (e.g., "I'm losing control," "I'm going to have a heart attack," "I'm going crazy," etc.) that intensify the panic symptoms.

33. Instruct the patient in using positive, realistic, self-assuring automatic thoughts (e.g., "If I relax and breathe deeply and slowly, this will pass," "I can control this experience," "Nobody dies from panic symptoms," etc.) that can replace distorted, negative thinking.

34. Teach the patient through modeling and behavioral rehearsal, the use of controlled, deep breathing to implement at the time of anxiety onset.

35. Teach the patient relaxation techniques, from deep breathing to progressive muscle relaxation. If the patient is able to use imagery techniques, teach these with muscle relaxation.

36. Provide the patient with a personalized audiotape of

relaxation instructions and/or suggest the purchase of a relaxation videotape if he/she owns a VCR.

37. Explain and use "Situational In Vivo Exposure" (described in *Anxiety and Its Disorders: The Nature and Treatment of Anxiety and Panic,* by Barlow, 1988), reassuring the patient that in vivo exposures are predictable and under his/her control.

38. Have the patient create a hierarchy of graduated approach to the feared objects or situations.

39. Instruct the patient to use his/her hierarchy of feared situations as a guide to repeatedly enter and remain in increasingly feared situations; encourage the use of coping skills (e.g., deep breathing, relaxation, and positive self-talk) and the presence of a friend, family member, or therapist as necessary.

40. Ask the patient to imagine the steps in the hierarchy of feared situations using systematic desensitization techniques.

41. Assist the patient in identifying the most effective personal stress management techniques from his/her past (e.g., prayer, walking, baking, telephoning a friend) and encourage daily scheduling of these activities.

42. Review healthy lifestyle issues with the patient (e.g., diet, exercise, caffeine and nicotine consumption, pleasurable activities, giving to others, etc.) and assist in developing a plan to eliminate anxiety producers, such as caffeine, and improve general wellness.

43. Perform or refer for a chemical dependence evaluation. (See the Substance Dependence/Misuse chapter in this *Planner.*)

44. Treat or refer for treatment of substance abuse. (See the Substance Dependence/Misuse chapter in this *Planner.*)

45. Teach the patient the concept of matching an individual's capacities and the demands of the physical environment (e.g., a frail elder taking care of a large house becomes overwhelmed).

46. Help the patient to determine if the current living situation is appropriate to his/her capacity, or if a change is warranted given current or anticipated capacity.

47. Assist the patient with the psychological aspects of changing his/her living situation (e.g., thinking about alternatives, choosing, planning, grieving losses, adapting, etc.).

48. Help the patient to determine if additional help is

needed to accomplish the Activities of Daily Living or the Instrumental Activities of Daily Living.

49. Refer the patient to aging services to obtain additional supports, such as the Area Agency on Aging, faith-based aging services, private geriatric care management, or other community services as available.

50. Discuss the patient's willingness to involve informal support network (e.g., family members, neighbors, religious counselors) in providing additional care and services; develop a plan to ask for help.

51. Help the patient determine which situations, events, and people can be assertively changed to reduce stress; teach assertion techniques (e.g., "I" statements, active listening) and encourage use.

52. Refer the patient to a specialty clinic for anxiety disorders if symptoms persist at a level that significantly interferes with function or well-being.

___. _____

_____

___. _____

_____

___. _____

_____

DIAGNOSTIC SUGGESTIONS

Axis I: 300.01   Panic Disorder without Agoraphobia
300.21   Panic Disorder with Agoraphobia
300.22   Agoraphobia without History of Panic Disorder
300.29   Specific Phobia
300.23   Social Phobia

_____   _____

_____   _____

PHYSICAL/SEXUAL/FINANCIAL ABUSE

BEHAVIORAL DEFINITIONS

1. Self-report of physical, sexual, or financial abuse by another.
2. Physical signs of abuse: bone fractures; skin wounds or bruises; blood; red, swollen, or torn genitalia; venereal disease.
3. Signs or reports of decreased or missing financial assets.
4. Unexplained change in mood and social behavior, with an increase in fearfulness, anxiety, distrust, depression, and/or anger.
5. Reports or concerns by staff or family caregivers that the patient seems unusually fearful, anxious, distressed, or guilty.
6. Refusing to be alone with specific friends, family members, staff, or other residents.
7. Increase in sexualized language or behaviors.
8. New onset of regressive behaviors (e.g., rocking, talking to self, wrapping self in a blanket).
9. New onset of sleep disturbance.
10. New onset of exit-seeking behavior.

__. _____

_____

__. _____

_____

__. _____

_____

LONG-TERM GOALS

1. Terminate the physical, sexual, or financial abuse.
2. Provide the patient with a safe environment, where his/her rights are fully respected.

3. Reduce or eliminate feelings of fear, anxiety, shame, and guilt.
4. Rebuild confidence in being protected and cared for.
5. Rebuild sense of safety and trust in others in the environment.
6. Reverse the pattern of increasing social withdrawal by slowly reengaging in activities.
7. Regain self-esteem and feelings of efficacy and control by giving testimony about abuse with support from others.

—. _____
   _____
   _____
—. _____
   _____
   _____
—. _____
   _____

SHORT-TERM OBJECTIVES

1. Comply with a medical evaluation and treatment. (1, 2, 3, 4)
2. Cooperate with a psychological evaluation. (5)
3. Describe the abuse incident(s) in as much detail as cognitive and emotional status allow. (6, 7, 8, 10, 11)
4. Identify the perpetrator with as much descriptive detail as cognitive and emotional status allow. (6, 7, 8, 9)
5. Identify and express the feelings connected to the abuse. (10, 11, 12, 13)
6. Verbalize fears about retaliation by the perpetrator or allies of the perpetrator. (9, 12, 14, 15, 16)
7. Verbalize guilt associated with ambivalent feelings

THERAPEUTIC INTERVENTIONS

1. Report abuse to the appropriate medical professionals, adult/elder protective agency, and residential administrators.
2. Follow applicable abuse reporting procedures as outlined in state and federal law and residential/agency policy.
3. Inform, or have appropriate person inform, the patient about abuse reporting procedures, providing reassurance, warmth, and support.
4. Arrange for an immediate medical assessment and treatment of the patient.
5. Conduct or refer for a psychological evaluation to determine emotional and cognitive status; convey results to primary physician.

toward the perpetrator and incidents, if they met needs for attention and love. (12, 17, 18)

8. Verbalize underlying unmet needs that led to vulnerability to abuse. (19)

9. Verbalize realistic placement of responsibility on the perpetrator. (20)

10. Increase satisfaction of unmet emotional/social needs with increased social interactions and support services. (21)

11. Identify persons with whom the patient feels safe. (22)

12. Identify the residential conditions that would feel safe. (23)

13. Cooperate with a temporary increase in safe supervision to restore confidence in personal safety. (15, 16, 24)

14. Cooperate with a long-term plan to provide a safe environment, including moving to a different residential setting or changing caregivers. (25)

15. Explore feelings about telling other persons, including family members, friends, or other residents, about the abuse incident. (26, 27)

16. Attend a support group for abuse survivors. (28, 29)

17. Decide on a strategy for developing the appropriate emotional support while maintaining privacy. (29)

6. Actively build the level of trust with the patient in individual sessions through consistent eye contact, active listening, unconditional positive regard, and warm acceptance to help increase his/her ability to identify and express feelings.

7. Establish with the patient the limits of confidentiality and privacy.

8. Encourage and support the patient in giving a detailed verbal account of the abuse (i.e., nature, frequency, and duration).

9. Encourage and support the patient in identification of the perpetrator.

10. Remain alert to nonverbal communication or cues, particularly when the patient is cognitively compromised.

11. Reduce open-ended questions to multiple-choice or yes/no forced-choice if the cognitive status prohibits lengthy verbal accounts of abuse.

12. Encourage and support the patient in verbally expressing and clarifying feelings of hurt, fear, anger, anxiety, guilt, and shame associated with the abuse.

13. Use or refer the patient for creative arts therapy to provide him/her with the opportunity to nonverbally express and work through

18. Demonstrate a stabilized mood and decreased emotional intensity connected to the abuse. (30)

19. Maintain confidence in personal safety while gradually decreasing temporary supervision measures. (31)

20. Terminate verbalizations of excuses for the perpetrator. (20, 32, 33, 34)

21. Increase feelings of efficacy and control by giving testimony against the perpetrator. (35, 36)

22. Increase feelings of self-esteem by accepting the role as a protector of other elders from abuse. (37)

—. _____
   _____

—. _____
   _____

—. _____
   _____

feelings of hurt, fear, anger, anxiety, guilt, and shame.

14. Explore specific fears about retaliation by the perpetrator or allies of the perpetrator; help the patient determine the probability of actual occurrence.

15. If veracity of charges cannot be established due to cognitive impairment, assess the patient's emotional status, and recommend safety precautions and protections based on current emotional distress, regardless of the legal resolution of abuse charges.

16. If the probability of retaliation is nonexistent, reassure the patient; if there is a possibility of retaliation, help the patient and/or family/staff problem-solve protections against retaliation.

17. Explore complex feelings about the perpetrator other than fear: loss/sadness, affection, betrayal, desire, anger, guilt, and so forth.

18. Validate the patient's ambivalent feelings.

19. Explore feelings and circumstances that left the patient vulnerable to abuse, including his/her feelings of loneliness, neglect, desire, confusion, or need for help.

20. Help the patient resolve feelings of guilt and responsibility, and reinforce the placement of responsibility on the perpetrator.

21. Discuss with the patient ways of having needs met (e.g., increasing social contact, home health care visitation, more family support, etc.) that do not leave him/her vulnerable to designing or abusive people.

22. Elicit from the patient a listing of persons (e.g., staff, family, neighbors, friends, etc.) with whom he/she feels safe; if cognitively impaired, have the patient point out people or pictures of people who are safe or not safe.

23. Elicit from the patient, with the help of a proxy decision-maker if necessary, residential conditions that feel safe (e.g., moving from a private home to a senior apartment, moving to a different floor of a nursing home, moving to a different facility, staying in the same residence but with a private-duty companion, etc.).

24. Arrange for an immediate increase in protection and supervision (e.g., change of locks on home, moving in with a relative, private-duty companion, being moved closer to the nursing station, respite care in an assisted living facility, etc.).

25. Facilitate conjoint sessions or discussions among the patient and involved others (family members, facility administrator, adult/elder protection agency, etc.) to

develop and implement a long-term plan for a safe residential environment that also maximizes the patient's autonomy.

26. Explore with the patient the balance of maintaining personal privacy and gaining emotional and social support.

27. Explain to the patient the possible benefits of discussing abuse more openly: gaining support, educating others, effecting policy changes.

28. Explore with the patient feelings about and opportunities for joining an appropriate support group for abuse survivors to decrease sense of isolation.

29. Develop a plan with the patient to pursue opportunities for support and interpretation of the experience, while maintaining the desired level of privacy.

30. Ask the patient to review the abuse incident again and reinforce greater control of emotions and a greater sense of empowerment and safety.

31. Arrange for conjoint sessions with involved others to discuss, decide upon, and implement a time frame for reducing temporary extra supervision measures; ensure the patient a sense of security during the transition.

32. Confront the patient about making excuses for the perpetrator's abuse.

33. Assign the patient to write a letter to the perpetrator and process it with the therapist.

34. Assign the patient to write a letter to other elders, warning them about perpetrators of abuse and process it with the therapist.

35. Provide support and reinforcement for the patient to follow through on abuse charges with legal action, stressing how he/she is protecting other vulnerable elders with such actions.

36. Arrange for concrete services (through social service, elder abuse, or victim service agencies) to reinforce cooperation with the legal system, such as transportation to, and personal support in, court.

37. Encourage the patient, as able, to become an advocate for elders who are victimized by designing or abusive people.

__. _____

_____

__. _____

_____

__. _____

_____

DIAGNOSTIC SUGGESTIONS

Axis I:	290.xx	Dementia of the Alzheimer's Type or Vascular Dementia
	780.09	Delirium NOS
	298.8	Brief Psychotic Disorder
	296.xx	Major Depressive Disorder
	300.4	Dysthymic Disorder
	309.81	Posttraumatic Stress Disorder
	308.3	Acute Stress Disorder
	300.02	Generalized Anxiety Disorder
	309.xx	Adjustment Disorder
	995.81	Physical/Sexual Abuse of Adult (Focus on Victim)
	————	————————————————
	————	————————————————

RESIDENTIAL ISSUES UNRESOLVED

BEHAVIORAL DEFINITIONS

1. Inability to manage daily activities required to maintain household because of physical and/or cognitive impairments.
2. Emotional distress caused by feelings of being overwhelmed by household management.
3. Living in the current residence poses danger to self or others because of fire hazards, physical or cognitive impairment, malnutrition, infestations, crime victimization, or abuse.
4. Family conflict regarding what is an appropriate living situation.
5. Inability to initiate the process of moving in spite of decision to do so.
6. Grief associated with loss of home.
7. Financial inability to maintain household.
8. Loneliness and social isolation associated with current residence (e.g., not wheelchair-accessible, not near public transportation, dislikes eating alone, etc.)

__. _____

_____

__. _____

_____

__. _____

_____

LONG-TERM GOALS

1. Match residential environment to physical, emotional, and cognitive needs and abilities.

2. Resolve emotional issues associated with residence: grief if a move is required, loss of independence and privacy if household help is added.
3. Resolve family conflict regarding residential status.
4. Ensure safe and comfortable residential environment.
5. Ensure adequate socialization opportunities within or outside the home.
6. Maximize the financial status through the use of creative home-financing mechanisms and the use of available senior services.

—. _____

_____

—. _____

_____

—. _____

_____

SHORT-TERM OBJECTIVES

1. Verbalize distress about the current living situation. (1, 2, 3)
2. Verbalize an understanding of the residential services and living options available. (4, 5)
3. Make a commitment to participate in, and cooperate with, the problem-solving process. (6)
4. Give consent for the therapist to contact family members, physicians, lawyer, social service, and aging agencies as needed. (7)
5. List concerns about the neighborhood that affect thoughts about the living situation. (8)

THERAPEUTIC INTERVENTIONS

1. Explore feelings of fear associated with the current or future residence, powerlessness, confusion, humiliation from the failure to maintain the home, anger toward the family, dread at leaving familiar surroundings, friends, and so forth.
2. Encourage the patient to confront the difficult issue of an appropriate residence head-on, and thereby stay in control of the decision making.
3. Reassure the patient that when the living environment (current home or new residence) matches his/her needs, abilities, and preferences, distress will decrease

6. Identify physical health limitations that cause problems with the current residence. (9)

7. Acknowledge cognitive functioning deficits that contribute to danger of the current living situation. (10)

8. Identify the emotional factors that make a change in residence very difficult. (11)

9. State the financial concerns that are exerting an influence on the housing decision. (12)

10. Identify the family dynamics that cause conflicts about residential decision making. (13)

11. For problems caused by health/strength and cognitive impairments, identify possible home modifications to adapt the home to the impairment. (14, 15)

12. State whether home modifications would address problems sufficiently so that continued residence is possible and desirable. (16)

13. Verbalize a resolution of the emotional distress related to a change in residence. (1, 17, 18)

14. Verbalize any problems that cannot be sufficiently addressed in the current residence. (19)

15. Verbalize acceptance of the necessity for alternative housing. (20)

and life satisfaction will return.

4. Describe the continuum of elder housing/service options: in-home services, adult day services, active adult/retirement living, senior apartment living, assisted living, nursing home, and continuing care retirement community.

5. Explain to the patient, without too much detail at first, that some creative financing options are available for those who want to remain in their homes, such as reverse mortgages.

6. Ask the patient to make a commitment to work on resolving the questions about the living situation, and the associated emotional issues.

7. Discuss with the patient the desirability of involving all interested parties in the decision-making process; ask for consent to contact particular individuals as necessary. Discuss limits of privacy and confidentiality.

8. Help the patient identify neighborhood contributions to the residence problem (crime, drugs, lack of public transportation, or shopping).

9. Assist the patient in identifying physical limitations (e.g., two or three stories, lack of grab-bars in the tub, kitchen cabinets too high,

16. Gather information with family members regarding alternative housing. (21)

17. Identify the relative benefits of staying near friends/neighbors versus moving near children/family. (22)

18. Discuss alternative residence options with family members. (23)

19. Give permission to the therapist to discuss housing and level of supervision requirements with family members. (24)

20. Review financial data to determine an appropriate strategy for financial analysis and planning. (25)

21. Cooperate with full financial/legal planning as appropriate for resources. (26)

22. Involve the family as needed/desired in developing a financial/residential plan. (27, 28)

23. Write a long-range residential plan that will maximize financial resources and opportunities, ensure a safe and comfortable living environment, and comply with all laws and regulations. (29)

24. Communicate the completed plan to family members. (30)

25. For problems caused by family dynamics, consent to family session(s) as needed. (31)

yard too big to maintain, house too big, needs major repairs, heating/cooling inadequate, etc.) that contribute to problems with the living situation.

10. Help the patient identify cognitive issues (e.g., leaves pots on stove, gets lost, wanders outside at night, etc.) that contribute to the housing problem.

11. Explore the emotional issues (e.g., can't leave home associated with deceased spouse, neighbors, childhood home, pets, etc.) that keep the patient from making an objective decision about housing and supervision needs.

12. Help the patient identify financial worries (e.g., resources tied up in home equity, can't afford assisted care) that are involved in the decision regarding a residence.

13. Explore the family dynamics (doesn't want to be dependent/a burden, doesn't want to stimulate family conflict, one spouse needs more care than the other, etc.) that influence decisions regarding the living situation.

14. Refer the patient to available counseling services (e.g., Area Agency on Aging, faith-based family services, Alzheimer's Association, occupational/physical ther-

26. In family sessions, verbalize short- and long-term goals and preferences for residence, level of independence, and amount of family contact. (32)

27. Ask directly for help—physical, emotional, or financial—from the family if desired. (33)

28. Verbalize an understanding of the family members' perspectives on residence, independence, finances, and amount of contact. (34, 35, 36)

29. Family members reach consensus on a written plan regarding residence, finances, and contact; specify who is responsible for what action at what time. (37)

30. Implement a residential plan, verbalizing emotional reactions during the process and asking for/receiving support as necessary. (38)

—. _____
   _____

—. _____
   _____

—. _____
   _____

apy departments of rehabilitation services) regarding home modifications and in-home services for physical and cognitive impairments.

15. Provide the patient with reading material, or refer to the library or bookstore offerings, regarding home modifications and in-home services.

16. Review possible home modifications. Consider grab-bars, stair-glides, reaching tools, substitution of timed electrical cooking equipment (e.g., microwaves or toaster ovens for gas or electric stoves) and services (e.g., homemaker, home health aides, handyman) and determine if addition of modifications/services would make remaining in the home environment feasible.

17. Review the patient's positive memories and current challenges about home environment.

18. Help the patient to complete the appropriate therapeutic process related to resolution of emotional distress (e.g., grief, anger, depression, anxiety, interpersonal conflict, etc.) caused by a change in residence.

19. Work with the patient to determine if problems related to physical limitations, cognitive deficits,

safety factors, and finances can be sufficiently resolved within the current residence.

20. If significant problems cannot be resolved, help the patient begin the process of considering alternative housing.

21. Assist the patient/family in gathering information about all possible housing alternatives, both near the current residence (and near friends, neighbors, and church) and near the children or other family members. Refer to community and faith-based resources for information.

22. Engage the patient in consideration of the relative merits of staying near the original home versus moving near the children/family versus moving for location desirability.

23. Encourage the patient to begin open discussions with the children/family about moving options.

24. With the patient's consent, contact family members to elicit their preferences and willingness to offer alternatives.

25. Assign the patient to gather basic financial data on assets and liabilities to determine the best strategy for planning the financial aspects of housing.

26. Based on relative complexity and strength of basic financial resources, suggest resources (e.g., certified financial planner or broker, personal or eldercare attorney, aging or social services case manager, personal banking services) to the patient for planning the financial aspects of residential living.

27. If cognitively capable, ask the patient to gather further information from friends, family, and reading; instruct the patient to discuss professional recommendations with friends/family.

28. Clarify with the patient to what extent family involvement is needed/desired in developing a residential plan.

29. Have the patient, with the help of family/professionals as needed or desired, develop a written long-term residential plan that addresses current problems and helps him/her achieve goals; addresses anticipated future problems and goals; and addresses possible complications, such as unanticipated health problems.

30. Encourage the patient to distribute copies of the completed plan to all interested parties, offering to talk in more detail about it as necessary.

31. Ask for the patient's consent to contact family members for conjoint session(s).

32. Encourage the patient in family sessions to review the long-range residential plan, to honestly, but gently, state preferences for levels and types of independence and amount and type of family support and contact.

33. Assist the patient in openly asking for help as needed from family members, knowing that all requests cannot necessarily be met, but that family members must be informed about the patient's need.

34. Encourage each family member to openly state his/her ability to provide support, including financial, physical, and emotional.

35. Reinforce to the family members that all types of support are valuable and welcome and that it is important for siblings to support each other as well as the parent(s).

36. Teach family members that under stressful conditions, eldercare can bring up old childhood rivalries and other feelings; that caregiving children may need to get support for themselves, including help with dealing with these childhood emotions.

37. Encourage the family to write out a plan to support

the elder's residential plan; be specific to prevent tension among siblings in the future.

38. Support the patient in the implementation of the residential plan; monitor and help with emotional reactions during the process; adapt the plan as necessary; and encourage the patient to continue asking for support as necessary.

—. _____
_____

—. _____
_____

—. _____
_____

DIAGNOSTIC SUGGESTIONS

Axis I: 290.xx   Dementia of the Alzheimer's Type or Vascular Dementia
780.09   Delirium NOS
293.9   Mental Disorder NOS Due to (Axis III Disorder)
296.xx   Major Depressive Disorder
300.4   Dysthymic Disorder
308.3   Acute Stress Disorder
300.02   Generalized Anxiety Disorder
309.xx   Adjustment Disorder

_____   _____
_____   _____

SEXUALLY INAPPROPRIATE/ DISINHIBITED BEHAVIOR

BEHAVIORAL DEFINITIONS

1. Grabbing, fondling, or holding the breasts or genitals of staff person providing personal care.
2. Unwelcome sexual remarks to staff person(s).
3. Masturbation in public areas.
4. Urinating into inappropriate containers (such as plants or radiators) or onto the floor.
5. Undressing in public areas.
6. Fondling or touching the genitals of unsuspecting persons.
7. Unpredictable episodes of aggression that seem to be independent of external stimulus conditions.
8. Impulsive actions, such as picking up and taking anything that looks appealing, or drinking dangerous fluids (such as cleaning supplies) or eating inedible/dangerous substances.

—. _____
_____

—. _____
_____

—. _____
_____

LONG-TERM GOALS

1. Reduce intensity and frequency of sexually inappropriate/ disinhibited behaviors.
2. Increase the safety of self, caregivers, and other persons in the environment.

3. Reduce stimuli, or triggers, of inappropriate behavior in the environment.

4. Increase stimuli, or triggers, for appropriate sexual behavior in private areas.

5. Staff/family caregivers improve capacity for managing behavior and gently redirecting.

6. Staff/family decrease angry, emotional reactions to disinhibited behavior, and understand these behaviors as part of the dementia process.

—. _____

_____

—. _____

_____

—. _____

_____

SHORT-TERM OBJECTIVES

1. Consent to participate in an evaluation of inappropriate behavior if decisionally capable; surrogate consents if the patient is not decisionally capable. (1)

2. Cooperate with the necessary safety precautions to protect self and others from harm. (2)

3. Cooperate with an evaluation to identify medical, neuropsychological, and/or psychological causative factors of the inappropriate behavior. (3, 4, 5, 6)

4. Complete treatment for confounding or coexisting depression, anxiety, medical

THERAPEUTIC INTERVENTIONS

1. Obtain consent from the patient or surrogate to address the problem of inappropriate behavior, including consent to discuss issues with other involved parties (e.g., family, staff, and physician).

2. Evaluate the severity of danger to self and others; take immediate safety precautions as needed (e.g., removing all toxic materials and sharp objects; putting childproof locks on food, medicine, and supply cabinets; etc.).

3. Refer to a physician for an evaluation of medical condi-

conditions, and/or adverse drug reactions. (6)

5. Cooperate with an evaluation to identify the specific behavioral pattern, if any, of the inappropriate behavior. (7, 8, 9)

6. Caregiver identifies possible antecedents to (trigger for) the patient's inappropriate behavior. (9, 10)

7. Caregiver ensures safety and dignity of the patient, other residents/family members, and himself/herself. (11, 12)

8. Satisfy tactile needs and bodily functions in an appropriate manner. (13)

9. Report feeling more accepted and attended to. (14)

10. Terminate inappropriate sexual behavior during personal care. (15)

11. Conduct sexual self-stimulation and/or toileting behaviors in private, appropriate locations. (13, 16, 17, 18, 19)

12. Consent to removal or substitution of sexually arousing items from public living areas. (20)

13. Express sex and affection desires in an appropriate manner with a willing partner. (21, 22, 23)

14. Increase appropriate physical activity/exercise and decrease impulsive aggressive activity. (24, 25, 26, 27, 28)

tions and medications (prescribed and OTC) that could be causing inappropriate behavior.

4. Conduct or refer for a psychological evaluation to assess possible contributions of depression, anxiety, substance use, premorbid personality, or coping styles.

5. Conduct or refer for a neurological and/or a neuropsychological evaluation to determine if the behavior is caused by his/her inability to inhibit behavior due to brain disorder.

6. Discuss the results of the evaluations with the patient, family, physician, and staff as appropriate; develop a plan to address treatable medical and psychological causes for the behavior.

7. Teach caregivers (family and/or staff) to keep behavioral records, establishing at least one week of baseline recording, or longer if episodes are infrequent.

8. Obtain or create a chart for caregivers to record baseline data; provide instruction on and motivation for proper recording of data.

9. Conduct a behavioral analysis, gathering detailed data on the frequency of the episodes, time of day, location, precipitants, specific behavior, consequences, and who was present.

15. Engage in activities and use materials that are familiar, and report positive memories and a feeling of being useful. (29, 30, 31, 32)

16. Engage in nonsexual but mutually pleasurable and satisfying activity with the caregiver. (33, 34)

17. Caregiver reports feeling supported and able to enjoy the benefits, as well as enduring the burdens of, the caregiver role. (33, 34, 35, 36)

—. _____
   _____

—. _____
   _____

—. _____
   _____

10. Analyze with caregivers the behavioral patterns, developing hypotheses about possible triggers of inappropriate behavior.

11. Analyze with caregivers the early warning signs of inappropriate behavior, if any.

12. Teach caregivers to ensure the safety and dignity of the patient, themselves, and others: react to disinhibited behavior with clear limits, but not harshly or critically; remove the patient from the environment if necessary.

13. Teach caregivers to address the patient's physical needs: toileting regularly; providing appropriate tactile stimulation, such as holding hands, or giving a stuffed animal to hold.

14. Teach caregivers to address the patient's emotional needs: spend at least five minutes talking; reassure the patient that he/she is accepted; reward warmly for appropriate behavior.

15. Teach caregivers to avoid overstimulating the patient during personal care: be kind but matter-of-fact; try a different caregiver (change from male/female); provide nonsexual tactile distraction items.

16. Teach caregivers to label the environment clearly: put a picture of a bed at the bedroom entrance and a pic-

ture of a toilet at the bathroom entrance.

17. Teach caregivers that dementia, not patient choice, causes inappropriate behavior; respond without undue attention, but matter-of-factly (e.g., "We don't do/say that here.") give an alternative appropriate location for private behavior (e.g., masturbate in your bedroom; urinate in the toilet; etc.).

18. Teach caregivers: don't argue back; don't scold or humiliate the patient; try not to convey your own anxiety or embarrassment.

19. Teach caregivers to help the patient associate the bedroom or bathroom with sexual activity by placing sexual photos in these private areas and saying, "This is where you can be private."

20. Teach caregivers to remove sexually arousing items from the patient's public living area; find substitutes for such items, if possible, that are not arousing.

21. Explore with the staff/family desires and opportunities for appropriate sexual expression, such as conjugal visits with spouse and/or appropriately expressed affection between residents.

22. Explain to the family and staff the complexity of decision making regarding sexuality when the patient is

cognitively impaired. (See the Decisional Incapacity Unresolved chapter in this *Planner.*)

23. Help the patient, staff, and family achieve a consensus on appropriate avenues for sexual expression.

24. Teach the staff/family that impulsive, unprovoked striking out can be a sign of the need for physical activity; occurrence might be reduced by providing more physical activity.

25. Encourage caregivers to brainstorm a list of all possible physical activities the patient could be engaged in: walking, beach ball toss, supervised exercise machine, and so forth.

26. Instruct caregivers to develop a schedule with as much daily physical activity as the patient is able to tolerate. Reinforce the patient's engaging in physical exercise.

27. Have caregivers keep a behavior log to record time spent in physical activity and inappropriate behaviors.

28. Help caregivers analyze behavior logs to determine if increasing physical activity is associated with a decrease in inappropriate behaviors.

29. Explore the patient's earlier life and the types of activi-

ties as to the materials that were most meaningful (e.g., accounting: adding machine, pencils, paper, etc.).

30. Assign caregivers to assemble a kit of materials from thrift shops or volunteers that represents satisfying parts of life work.

31. Instruct caregivers to provide time and space for the patient to engage in prior activities (e.g., using an adding machine, sanding wood, using a flashlight, folding towels, etc.).

32. Instruct caregivers to spend time letting the patient reminisce, using familiar objects from earlier in life.

33. Assign the patient and caregivers to develop a list of mutually satisfying, pleasurable, feasible activities (e.g., looking at photographs, grooming nails, feeding birds, etc.).

34. Instruct the patient and caregiver to engage in one mutually satisfying, pleasurable activity per day together.

35. Encourage caregivers to care for themselves: get social support; use respite care; manage stress with diet, exercise, tension reduction, and caregiver education/support groups.

36. Recommend to the facility that staff caregivers be provided with a support group.

—.   _____
     _____
—.   _____
     _____
—.   _____
     _____

DIAGNOSTIC SUGGESTIONS

Axis I:
	293.0	Delirium Due to (Axis III Disorder)
	291.0	Alcohol Intoxication or Withdrawal Delirium
	292.0	Sedative, Hypnotic, or Anxiolytic Withdrawal
	292.81	Other or Unknown Substance-Induced Delirium
	290.xx	Dementia of the Alzheimer's Type or Vascular Dementia, with Behavioral Disturbance
	294.1	Dementia Due to (Head Trauma, Parkinson's Disease, Huntington's Disease, or Axis III Disorder)
	290.10	Dementia Due to Pick's Disease or Creutzfeldt-Jakob Disease
	294.8	Dementia NOS
	291.2	Alcohol-Induced Persisting Dementia
	294.9	Cognitive Disorder NOS
	995.2	Adverse Effects of Medication NOS
	310.1	Personality Change Due to (Axis III Disorder), Disinhibited Type
	309.3	Adjustment Disorder with Disturbance of Conduct

_____   _____
_____   _____

SLEEP DISTURBANCE

BEHAVIORAL DEFINITIONS

1. Difficulty getting to sleep or maintaining sleep.
2. Sleeping adequately but not feeling refreshed or rested after waking.
3. Increased sleep latency (time it takes to fall asleep), wake time after sleep onset, or number of night awakenings.
4. Increased number of daytime naps.
5. Regular, ongoing use of sleeping medication.
6. Sleep-wake pattern reversal.
7. Nocturnal wandering.

__. _____
   _____
__. _____
   _____
__. _____
   _____

LONG-TERM GOALS

1. Restore a restful sleep pattern.
2. Feel refreshed and energetic during wakeful hours.
3. Eliminate regular use of sleeping medication.
4. Return to a normal, restful sleep pattern results in reduced stress on caregiver by improving caregiver's ability to obtain sleep.
5. Resolve underlying physiological and psychological contributions to poor sleep pattern.

—. _____
_____
_____

—. _____
_____
_____

—. _____
_____

SHORT-TERM OBJECTIVES

1. Verbalize the problems with sleep disturbance. (1, 2)

2. Consent to participate in medical and psychological evaluations of sleep disturbance if decisionally capable; surrogate consents if the patient is not decisionally capable. (2, 3)

3. Cooperate with necessary safety precautions. (3, 4, 5, 6)

4. Cooperate with an evaluation to identify physiological or psychological causative factors of the sleep disturbance. (7, 8, 9)

5. Complete the treatment for confounding or coexisting depression, anxiety, sleep apnea, restless leg syndrome, and/or adverse drug reactions. (9)

6. Record sleep variables in a daily diary. (10)

7. Implement sleep hygiene related to consistent sleep rhythm. (11)

8. Cooperate with recommendations regarding ingestion

THERAPEUTIC INTERVENTIONS

1. Ask the patient to discuss specific complaints about sleep and how disturbance in sleep is affecting everyday functioning and interpersonal relationships.

2. Reassure the patient that sleep problems are common with advancing age, but that medical and behavioral interventions have demonstrated efficacy in improving sleep patterns.

3. Obtain consent from the patient or surrogate to address the problem of sleep disturbance, including consent to discuss issues with other involved parties, such as the family, staff, and physician.

4. Evaluate the severity of danger to self during nocturnal wakening period: number of falls, exit-seeking behaviors, ingestion of inappropriate food or substances.

5. Review basic safety precautions with the patient and

of food, medication, and liquids. (12)

9. Get physical exercise in the late afternoon. (13)

10. Verbalize satisfaction with the sleep environment. (14)

11. Engage in sleep-inducing activities in the evening. (15)

12. Get out of bed when not sleeping for 20 minutes. (16, 17, 18)

13. Establish and consistently repeat a presleep ritual. (19)

14. Practice deep-muscle relaxation exercises. (20)

15. Use biofeedback training to deepen relaxation skill. (21)

16. Comply with an individualized sleep compression schedule. (22, 23)

17. Report regularly on successes and problems with sleep hygiene, stimulus control, and sleep compression. (24, 25, 26)

18. Verbalize an improvement in the sleep pattern. (27, 28, 29)

19. Cooperate with sleep clinic referral and evaluation. (30)

—. _____
_____

—. _____
_____

—. _____
_____

caregiver: remove area rugs; keep walking path (e.g., to the bathroom) obstacle-free; install nightlights and safety locks on cabinet doors with medicines, toxic materials, or inappropriate food; install a stair safety gate; have the patient wear an identification bracelet; keep doors locked; install door alarms.

6. Assess whether nocturnal behavior currently poses such a significant threat to patient safety or caregiver well-being that immediate measures are necessary (such as a move to a more secure location or sleeping medication), or whether more deliberate behavioral approaches can be tried.

7. Refer to the physician for an evaluation of medical conditions (such as sleep apnea or restless leg syndrome) or medications that could be causing or contributing to impaired sleep patterns.

8. Conduct or refer for a psychological evaluation to assess possible contributions of depression and/or anxiety to sleep disturbance.

9. Discuss the results of the evaluations with the patient, family, physician, and staff as appropriate; develop a plan to address

treatable medical and psychological causes for the sleep disturbance. (See the Depression or Anxiety chapters in this *Planner.*)

10. Assign the patient or caregiver to keep a daily sleep diary including: time to bed; time fell asleep; number of awakenings; length of each awakening; reason for awakening; time awoke in the morning; time of arising; number of naps; minutes per nap; a 1-to-5 rating of how refreshed upon awakening and how restful the sleep was; type and dosage of sleep medication.

11. Teach the patient or caregiver three rules of sleep hygiene designed to develop a consistent sleep rhythm: Delay bedtime until drowsy and ready to sleep; rise or wake at the same time every morning, including weekends; try to avoid naps altogether, but if necessary, restrict to one hour before 1:00 P.M.

12. Teach the patient or caregiver rules of sleep hygiene related to substance ingestion: no alcohol within two hours of bedtime; no caffeine (from foods like chocolate, beverages, or medication) within six hours of bedtime; no nicotine within three hours of bedtime; no large amount of sugar or fluid just before

bedtime; take CNS stimulant or diuretic medications earlier than three hours before bedtime.

13. Discuss the importance of daily exercise with the patient or caregiver, especially if the patient is in a restless phase of a dementing illness. The optimal time for the beneficial effect of exercise on sleep is in the late afternoon. Avoid exercise after 6:00 P.M.

14. Discuss the sleep environment with the patient or caregiver, and help with problem solving to achieve comfortable levels of temperature, sound, light, and noise.

15. Encourage sleep-inducing activities like drinking warm milk, listening to restful music, enjoying relaxation exercises, etc.

16. Teach the patient or caregiver not to use the bed or bedroom for any activity other than sleep or sexual activity.

17. Teach the patient to increase association between bed and sleep by trying to go to sleep within 20 minutes of retiring; if unsuccessful, get out of bed and go to another room for music or reading until drowsy; return to bed to sleep.

18. Repeat training of association until sleep is achieved

within 20 minutes of retiring. Use the same procedure for nocturnal wakening. Do not stay awake in bed for longer than 20 minutes.

19. Review with the patient or caregiver the activities 30 or 60 minutes prior to established bedtime: identify a defined ritual (e.g., watch the news, walk the dog, turn out some lights, set the alarm, bathroom/teeth/grooming, etc.); assign the patient or caregiver to follow ritual activities in the same order every night.

20. Train in deep-muscle relaxation exercises with or without audiotape instruction.

21. Administer electromyographic (EMG) biofeedback to reinforce successful relaxation response.

22. Using sleep diary information, identify an amount of time to be spent in bed that is less than the amount currently spent in bed, but not more than eight hours (six to seven hours would be typical, but up to eight hours may be necessary to accommodate patient/caregiver needs or advanced age).

23. Negotiate with the patient or caregiver a bedtime and rising time that would incorporate the compressed sleep schedule.

24. Assign the patient to continue the daily sleep diary, now noting any deviation from the sleep hygiene and stimulus control rules and the sleep compression schedule.

25. Assign the patient to write comments down on the daily sleep diary about reasons for deviations, suggestions for change, and feelings or thoughts about the therapeutic procedure.

26. Review deviations from the rules and schedule and problem-solve with the patient to modify as necessary.

27. Construct a chart for the patient or caregiver to visually display progress in sleep behaviors (minutes to sleep onset, number and length of nocturnal wakings, minutes between morning waking and rising), and/or outcomes (ratings of refreshed feelings, ratings of restful sleep, medication usage).

28. Explain to the patient or caregiver that often sleep initially gets worse before it gets better, and that changing ingrained patterns is hard but manageable.

29. Negotiate modifications of the plan with the patient, continually using sleep diary (with daily comments as well as statistics) as a

basis to monitor progress and deviations from plan.

30. Refer to a sleep clinic for an assessment of sleep apnea or other physiological factors if sleep disturbance persists.

___. _____
     _____

___. _____
     _____

___. _____
     _____

DIAGNOSTIC SUGGESTIONS

Axis I:
307.42	Primary Insomnia
780.59	Breathing-Related Sleep Disorder
307.45	Circadian Rhythm Sleep Disorder
307.47	Dyssomnia NOS
307.42	Insomnia Related to . . . (Indicate Axis I Disorder)
780.52	Sleep Disorder, Insomnia Type, Due to (Axis III Disorder)
291.8	Alcohol-Induced Sleep Disorder
292.89	Sedative-, Hypnotic-, or Anxiolytic-Induced Sleep Disorder
_____	_____
_____	_____

SOMATIZATION

BEHAVIORAL DEFINITIONS

1. Heightened sensitivity to bodily distress and frequent contact with health care providers.
2. Reports of physical symptoms (such as pain, gastrointestinal distress, shortness of breath, or fatigue) that suggest a medical condition, but are not fully explained by a general medical condition.
3. Significant impairment in daily functioning or significant distress caused by unexplained physical symptoms.
4. Continuing use of multiple physicians, other health professionals, laboratory tests, surgeries, medications and remedies related to unexplained physical symptoms.
5. Continual requests to be seen by the physician or nurse, in spite of a physician determination that no further medical evaluations are necessary.
6. Preoccupation with the concern that one has a serious disease, in spite of objective medical evidence to the contrary.
7. Physician determination that psychological factors are affecting the onset, severity, exacerbation, or maintenance of pain.
8. Adoption of the patient role as the predominant social role, with attendant degradation of role functioning as a family member, friend, employee, volunteer, citizen, or member of a religious congregation.

—. _____

_____

—. _____

_____

—. _____

_____

LONG-TERM GOALS

1. Recognize and resolve underlying or masked depression or anxiety.
2. Modify unrealistic health goals, such as being free from all pain or being absolutely certain about medical diagnoses.
3. Shift the focus of attention from diagnosis and cure to managing and minimizing the impact of physical symptoms.
4. Improve daily functioning and feelings of well-being in spite of some remaining physical symptoms or doubts.
5. Reestablish good working relationships with health care providers.
6. Reduce inappropriate use of medical services.

—. _____
_____
—. _____
_____
—. _____
_____

SHORT-TERM OBJECTIVES

1. Identify the specific most disturbing or disruptive physical symptoms and their meaning or importance. (1, 2, 3)
2. Verbalize an understanding that all symptoms are real and that the physician's referral for psychotherapy is not a negative judgment or rejection. (4, 5, 6)
3. Verbalize an understanding of the multiple causes of physical symptoms and the multiple approaches that can help resolve the issues. (7, 8, 9, 10)
4. Give written consent for the referring physician(s) and

THERAPEUTIC INTERVENTIONS

1. Assign the patient to verbalize or list all specific physical symptoms in detail and to rank-order the symptoms on the basis of how disturbing they are.
2. Help the patient to identify whether and/or how each symptom interferes with daily functioning and/or relationships.
3. Assist the patient in identifying the meaning or importance of each physical symptom (e.g., chest pain may be disturbing as pain, as a sign of stress, or as an impending heart attack).

designated family members to be contacted. (11, 12)

5. Keep a daily journal of physical symptoms for one week to establish a baseline. (13, 14)

6. Compile a list of all medical conditions, approximate date of diagnosis, and the treating physician(s). (15)

7. Compile a list of all prescribed and over-the-counter medications, dosage, and time of day they are taken. (16)

8. Comply with a psychological evaluation to identify underlying emotional distress, premorbid personality factors, or coping styles that could be interacting with physical symptoms. (17)

9. Comply with a neuropsychological evaluation to identify cognitive factors that could be contributing to symptom presentation or could influence the psychotherapy process. (18)

10. Give informed consent to treatment for underlying emotional distress. (19)

11. List goals for treatment. (20)

12. Modify beliefs to more realistic assumptions about physical distress. (21, 22, 23)

13. Agree to negotiated goals as part of the treatment plan. (24, 25)

14. Accept a referral to a geropsychiatrist, psychiatrist, or other physician. (26)

4. Reassure the patient that all symptoms are a legitimate focus of concern, and that the patient will not be rejected or dismissed if no firm biological basis to the distress is found.

5. Validate the patient's distress caused by the physical symptoms to advance the working treatment alliance.

6. Reassure the patient that the referral from the physician to the therapist does not mean that the physician has given up on the patient; therapist and physician will work closely together.

7. Explain that most symptoms, including pain, have psychological, social, and physical components (biopsychosocial model).

8. Teach the patient that some people have a biological vulnerability for heightened sensitivity or awareness of physical distress.

9. Instruct the patient on the fact that often people are taught to fear disease more than necessary; the extra fears or beliefs can be alleviated with more education.

10. Explain that part of the goal of treatment will be behavioral: recreating a satisfying lifestyle.

11. Discuss with the patient the necessity for working with the primary care physician and involved specialists.

15. Correct misinformation and exaggerated beliefs that lead to morbid fear of disease. (9, 21, 27, 28)

16. Reduce contact with the physician's office that stems from morbid, irrational fear of disease. (29, 30)

17. Identify instances of distorted cognitive processes, such as selective misperception and misattribution, that maintain fears of disease. (31)

18. Implement more realistic, positive automatic thoughts regarding symptoms. (32, 33)

19. Learn and practice relaxation techniques for fear and stress reduction. (34)

20. Identify the negative impact of the preoccupation with physical symptoms. (2, 35)

21. Increase the frequency of pleasurable and/or service activities. (36, 37)

22. Identify and problem-solve life transition stressors that provoke or exacerbate physical symptoms. (38)

23. Comply with a treatment schedule developed in conjunction with the treating physician(s). (39)

__. _____
   _____

__. _____
   _____

__. _____
   _____

Obtain written consent from the patient to speak with the physician.

12. Discuss with the patient the need or desire to involve designated family members in treatment. Obtain written consent to speak with family members as necessary.

13. Create a chart to record symptom frequency, intensity (rate 1 to 10), time of day, duration, as well as the situation, people, thoughts, moods, and behaviors that precede or follow the symptoms.

14. Assign the patient to complete the symptom chart on a daily basis.

15. Assign the patient to produce a list of all medical conditions, approximate date of diagnosis, and the treating physician(s).

16. Assign the patient to produce a list of all prescribed and over-the-counter medications, dosages, and times of day they are taken. If necessary, ask that all medication containers be brought to the next session.

17. Conduct or refer for a psychological evaluation to identify emotional distress, personality factors, or coping styles that could be contributing to physical symptom management.

18. Conduct or refer for a neuropsychological evaluation

to identify cognitive factors that could be contributing to symptom presentation or that could influence the psychotherapy process.

19. Seek the patient's commitment to treatment of the emotional distress that may be contributing to physical complaints.

20. Assign the patient to verbalize or write out personal goals for psychotherapy.

21. Teach the patient to change belief from "Pain or discomfort signals a diagnosable disease," to "Physical discomfort is common and usually has no serious medical cause."

22. Teach the patient to change belief from "Health is the absence of discomfort," to "Health is functioning and enjoying life in spite of some discomfort."

23. Teach the patient to change belief from "More tests will reveal an exact diagnosis," to "Symptoms are annoying, but more tests now won't help."

24. Discuss the goals of treatment, being realistic about what's possible to achieve (e.g., total resolution of symptoms is unlikely, but you could return to your volunteer job).

25. Decide on treatment goals and approach and share with the treating physi-

cian(s) for input and feedback.

26. Refer to a geropsychiatrist,
knowledgeable about the
use of antidepressants for
somatic disorders, espe-
cially pain and hypochon-
driasis.

27. In conjunction with the
physician, give the patient
simple, clear information
that logically explains why
exaggerated fear of disease
is unfounded.

28. Challenge the patient when
unreasonable fears emerge,
and teach the patient to
challenge himself/herself
with the correct informa-
tion; teach the patient
thought-stopping and dis-
traction techniques.

29. If exaggerated fears lead to
too frequent phone calls to
physician offices, jointly
develop a behavioral con-
tract with the physician,
office staff, and patient to
divert calls to the therapist.

30. Use behavioral contracting
and reinforcement scheduling to curtail inappropriate
calls.

31. Discuss the patient's
thought process moving
from symptom to fear of disease; identify instances of
selective misperception and
misattribution.

32. Teach and have the patient
practice alternative interpretations of the same phys-

ical symptom data that are more realistic and in line with physician analysis.

33. Provide positive reinforcement to the patient for cognitive restructuring and ignore expressions of disease fear.

34. Teach and monitor the patient's practice of deep breathing techniques, progressive muscle relaxation, and/or use of audio/video relaxation tapes. Encourage the use of relaxation techniques when fear and stress are present.

35. Review daily activities schedule with the patient, and determine whether somatic symptoms have caused a decrease in role function (other than sick/disabled role).

36. Have the patient list possible pleasurable activities that increase interpersonal contact, and/or contribute to welfare of others less fortunate.

37. Assign the patient to engage in one pleasurable or service-related activity each day.

38. Identify major life transitions or stressors that exacerbate physical symptoms. (See Life Role Transition chapter in this *Planner.*)

39. Help the physician develop a treatment schedule that includes: regular pre-

planned contact regardless
of symptoms, expression of
caring, validation of symptoms, and no unnecessary
tests, medications, or therapies.

—· _____

_____

—· _____

_____

—· _____

_____

DIAGNOSTIC SUGGESTIONS

Axis I: 300.81   Somatization Disorder
300.81   Undifferentiated Somatoform Disorder
307.xx   Pain Disorder
300.7   Hypochondriasis
300.81   Somatoform Disorder NOS
300.02   Generalized Anxiety Disorder
293.89   Anxiety Disorder Due to (Axis III Disorder)

_____   _____

_____   _____

SPIRITUAL CONFUSION

BEHAVIORAL DEFINITIONS

1. Verbalizes the loss of a sense of meaning or purpose in life.
2. Verbalizes anger at God or unjust world.
3. Expresses feelings of guilt and fears regarding not being forgiven by God or others for past misdeeds.
4. Expresses a desire for a closer relationship with God.
5. Death of a loved one or the patient's imminent death creates painful questioning of lifelong beliefs.
6. Verbalizes questions, fears, and concerns about life after death (e.g., Heaven, hell, salvation, condemnation, etc.).
7. Express distress due to unfinished business (e.g., desiring to mend a relationship or ask for forgiveness).
8. Verbalizes a need to make sense of life or see life in perspective.
9. Verbalizations focus solely on self; unable to experience concern for others or a relationship with higher power.
10. Unable to attend religious services due to inadequate transportation, moving into an assisted care living facility or nursing home.
11. Expresses desire to discuss spiritual concerns but perceives no opportunity to do so.

__. _____
_____

__. _____
_____

__. _____
_____

LONG-TERM GOALS

1. Alleviate feelings of depression and distress; achieve a feeling of being at peace.
2. Terminate feelings of guilt and feel a sense of forgiveness by God and/or others.
3. Reaffirm a sense of faith.
4. Express satisfaction from feeling meaningfully connected to something beyond self (e.g., other people, history, a higher power, etc.).
5. Express feelings of being able and/or ready to cope with the death of a loved one or of self.
6. Complete the steps necessary to resolve unfinished business.
7. Establish goals and satisfying activities for the remainder of life.
8. Achieve a satisfying perspective of the role of one's own life in the larger world.
9. Establish or reestablish opportunities for worship, prayer, and/or discussion of spiritual concerns.

__. _____
_____
__. _____
_____
__. _____
_____

SHORT-TERM OBJECTIVES

1. Verbalize the most pressing concerns that may be based in spiritual distress.
   (1, 2, 3)

2. Identify personally satisfying ways of coping with spiritual concerns throughout life and currently.
   (4, 5, 6)

3. Participate in problem solving to find new venues for spiritual expression, exploration, and comfort.
   (7, 8, 9, 10)

THERAPEUTIC INTERVENTIONS

1. Encourage the patient to verbalize deeper spiritual concerns that may underlie anxiety or depressive symptoms.

2. Directly question the patient about feelings, beliefs, and values associated with such issues as death and dying, religious convictions and beliefs, if any, in an afterlife.

3. Model comfort in discussing spiritual issues, and reas-

4. Express deepest feelings of anger, bitterness, confusion ("Why me?"), depression, and distress. (10, 11, 12, 13)

5. Verbalize feelings of comfort from having help from another to face spiritual challenges. (10, 14, 15)

6. Participate in a life review process. (16, 17)

7. Verbalize values and beliefs, and identify how they have developed and changed over time. (18)

8. Identify what is most important to accomplish in the remainder of life. (19, 20)

9. Participate in problem solving to develop a plan to accomplish goals. (21)

10. Begin implementation of a plan, monitor the results, identify and resolve the barriers, and continue implementation. (22, 23)

11. Learn and practice skills to communicate caring to others. (24, 25, 26)

12. Learn and practice recognition, acceptance, and appreciation of others' communication of caring toward the patient himself/herself. (27, 28, 29)

13. Identify moments in life when the patient achieved the experience of a satisfying, meaningful connection to a higher power. (30, 31)

14. Explore possibilities within the patient's life that could

sure the patient that these are appropriate topics for discussion to the extent that they are causing distress and/or interfering with function.

4. Explore patterns of thinking about and acting on spiritual concerns throughout the life span, noting what was most satisfying, when shifts occurred and why.

5. Ask the patient to describe current ways of thinking about and acting on spiritual concerns (e.g., going to church, praying, reading, meditation, appreciating nature, serving others, etc.).

6. Encourage the patient to identify and reflect on desired ways of coping with spiritual concerns and barriers to fulfilling those desires.

7. Brainstorm alternative ways to practice spirituality, such as arranging for a friend or volunteer to drive to church, having a chaplain visit, or trying a new type of worship service.

8. Ask a staff or family member, with the patient's permission, to provide spiritually oriented reading material that is congruent with the patient's belief system, in large print if necessary.

9. Ask a staff or family member, with the patient's per-

recapture a sense of spiritual connectedness. (32)

15. Develop and implement a plan to search for spiritual peace. (33, 34, 35, 36)

16. Identify spiritual distress or challenges created by the patient's own perceived imminent death or the dying of a loved one. (37)

17. Verbalize feelings, beliefs, and values raised by death or dying. (38)

18. Adapt beliefs and value system to accommodate new understandings and insights gained during death and the dying process. (39)

—. _____
   _____
—. _____
   _____
—. _____
   _____

mission, to help with finding and providing spiritually oriented audio/videotapes and TV programs that are congruent with the patient's belief system.

10. Ask a staff or family member, with the patient's permission, to arrange for regular, scheduled visits from a minister, priest, rabbi, or other spiritual advisor requested by the patient.

11. As the patient is willing and able, encourage sharing of the deepest negative feelings and existential questions, providing comfort and acceptance.

12. Support the patient through despair, reinforcing the process of becoming more fully human through confrontation with life's deepest mysteries.

13. Encourage the patient to ask *why,* and explain that answers will come from within, with the help of spiritual advisors, reading, meditation, praying, and so forth.

14. Explain that, while no one can take away spiritual pain, the patient will not have to endure pain alone; have the patient identify primary family, clergy, staff, and volunteer supports.

15. Provide comfort, security, acceptance, support, and a

sense of hope and confidence that the patient will find solace and gain wisdom.

16. Using active listening, gently guide the patient through the life review process, recounting feelings and events of different stages, and lessons learned.

17. Encourage the patient to keep a journal, make an audiotape, or write a letter, summarizing life events, observations, and wisdom gained through the years.

18. Work with the patient to identify core values that have emerged and remained throughout his/her life (i.e., What values does the patient use to guide life choices? How was that value system learned and supported?).

19. Ask the patient to identify what are the remaining goals to be accomplished in life? How do these goals reflect the patient's core values?

20. If some goals cannot be accomplished because of health or financial constraints, discuss with the patient alternative goals based on the same values.

21. Brainstorm with the patient ways to accomplish goals, using family, staff, religious and community resources as available.

22. Instruct the patient to implement a plan, monitor implementation, and identify and problem-solve barriers to implementation.

23. Help the patient modify goals as necessary to keep them realistic and achievable.

24. Share with the patient how verbal and nonverbal expression of love, service, caring, and appreciation to others can fulfill a common spiritual mandate.

25. Help the patient formulate comfortable ways to communicate caring to others.

26. Practice and role-play communication of caring and appreciative messages.

27. Review with the patient the people in life likely to communicate caring or positive messages to him/her.

28. Ask the patient to identify how each individual expresses caring, verbally or nonverbally, easily or with difficulty.

29. Teach and role-play with the patient the acknowledgment of and expression of gratitude for the caring messages from others.

30. Review the patient's life to search for moments of feeling connected to a higher power (e.g., through nature, music, reading religious material, prayer, etc.).

31. Discuss with the patient the perspective gained and the satisfaction of feeling less preoccupied with self.

32. Ask the patient to identify how those feelings of spiritual connectedness (e.g., communication and relationship with a higher power, peaceful reassurance, transcendence) might be achieved in the patient's current situation.

33. Help the patient identify and problem-solve ways around the barriers to achieving spiritual peace of mind in the current situation.

34. Encourage, advocate for, and arrange for situations (e.g., time and place for meditation and/or prayer, attendance at worship services, visits with clergy, audio- or videotape of spiritual material congruent with the patient's belief system) that promote the strengthening of the patient's spiritual faith and connection to a higher power.

35. Explore how the patient has served his/her higher power and/or fellow humans throughout his/her lifetime.

36. Reinforce the value of the patient's "gifts" (e.g., of time, caring, teaching, family heritage, etc.) no matter how small, to others.

37. Identify issues raised by death (e.g., "Why would God

be so cruel?" "I don't believe in an afterlife, but I can't tolerate the thought that I won't be with my wife again." "Will I go to Heaven after my death?" "Has God forgiven me for my sins?")

38. Help the patient explore the feelings, ambivalence, doubts, and contradictions in beliefs and values that are created by death or dying of himself/herself or a loved one. Refer the patient to his/her spiritual advisor for reassurance of beliefs and faith.

39. Support the patient through realignment of beliefs and value system to accommodate new insights and wisdom gained through the experience of death and dying; encourage the patient to find solace in promises inherent in his/her belief system.

__. _____
   _____

__. _____
   _____

__. _____
   _____

DIAGNOSTIC SUGGESTIONS

Axis I: 296.xx   Major Depressive Disorder
        300.4   Dysthymic Disorder
        311   Depressive Disorder NOS
        300.02   Generalized Anxiety Disorder

300.00	Anxiety Disorder NOS
309.xx	Adjustment Disorder
316	Psychological Factors Affecting Medical Condition
995.2	Adverse Effects of Medication NOS
290.21	Dementia of the Alzheimer's Type, with Depressed Mood
290.43	Vascular Dementia with Depressed Mood
————	————————————————
————	————————————————

SUBSTANCE DEPENDENCE/MISUSE

BEHAVIORAL DEFINITIONS

1. Continued use of a mood-altering substance after being told that using it is causing or contributing to health problems.
2. Increased tolerance for the substance shown by a need for an increasing amount to achieve the desired effect.
3. Withdrawal symptoms after cessation of use, such as sweating, hand tremor, insomnia, nausea, anxiety, or seizures.
4. Alcohol intoxication and/or medication misuse observed on two or more occasions.
5. Marked change in behavior, that is, withdrawal from family and close friends, a loss of interest in activities, low energy, or sleeping difficulty.
6. Unsteady gait or dizziness that result in frequent falling down.
7. Slurred speech.
8. Difficulties with driving, such as accidents or DUI charges.
9. Unpredictable mood swings.
10. Increasingly private or secretive behavior.
11. Inability or unwillingness to follow through with responsibilities or commitments.
12. Negative outlook on life, other people and self, including expressions of guilt or shame.

__. _____
   _____
__. _____
   _____
__. _____
   _____

LONG-TERM GOALS

1. Confirm or rule out the existence of substance dependence or abuse.
2. Determine the scope, severity, and cause of the substance problems.
3. Develop a plan to control or abstain from substance use.
4. Develop an understanding of the pattern of substance dependence and abuse.
5. Implement alternative strategies to cope with stress or loneliness to avoid relapse and sustain long-term recovery.
6. Identify and pursue relationships, groups, activities, and locations that will promote a healthy and satisfying lifestyle.

—. _____

_____

—. _____

_____

—. _____

_____

SHORT-TERM OBJECTIVES	THERAPEUTIC INTERVENTIONS
1. Acknowledge impairment in functioning and admit to the possible contributory role of substance misuse. (1, 2)	1. Discuss with the patient the current difficulties in functioning (physical, cognitive, social, or occupational), and how or whether the misuse or abuse of alcohol, sedatives/hypnotics/anxiolytics, and/or pain medications could be contributing to the functional impairment.
2. Identify the type and extent of substance use. (2)	
3. Explain the role that substance use/abuse plays in meeting identified needs. (2, 3)	
4. Verbalize an understanding of risks associated with the use of mood-altering substances. (4)	2. Explore with the patient the pattern of substance use.
5. Terminate the denial and take responsibility for substance abuse. (5)	3. Explore the patient's reasons for the perceived need for the substance, and willingness to consider alternative ways of meeting that need.

6. Identify feelings of shame and fear associated with substance abuse. (5, 6, 7)

7. Verbalize consent to involve a physician, and if appropriate, family or significant others, in an evaluation and treatment for substance misuse and the underlying causative factors. (8)

8. Complete a comprehensive evaluation for substance dependence. (9, 10)

9. Give a detailed history of substance use, including any stresses that trigger abuse. (11)

10. Describe, or family/staff describes, medication consumption regimen and any difficulties associated with recalling whether medications have been taken. (12)

11. Cooperate with the physician's recommendations regarding changes in medications or the restriction of their administration. (13)

12. Cooperate with a supervised detoxification process. (14)

13. Change the diet to a more healthy regimen. (15)

14. Use alternative positive behaviors to cope with problems such as pain, loneliness, or sleeplessness, and terminate the use of substance use/abuse to cope. (16)

15. Attend Alcoholics Anonymous meetings. (17)

4. Educate the patient about the appropriate use of addictive substances, the risks of substance misuse (e.g., increased tolerance, altered judgment, negative medication interactions, physical injury, depression exacerbation, etc.), and the potential to improve the quality of life by reducing or eliminating dependence on chemical substances.

5. Help the patient to acknowledge a personal responsibility for substance use, while not allowing him/her to become overwhelmed or immobilized by shame.

6. Help the patient to verbalize feelings of guilt and shame associated with substance misuse.

7. Encourage the patient's open discussion of substance misuse, showing that it leads to constructive problem solving.

8. Assign the patient to identify at least one other supportive individual (family member, physician, etc.) with whom to openly discuss substance problems.

9. Engage the patient in a hopeful vision of life that is not dependent on substance use; persuade that the first step is a comprehensive evaluation and care plan formulation.

10. Arrange for a complete evaluation of the patient:

16. Select and cooperate with the most appropriate level of supervised treatment to recover from a substance abuse pattern. (18, 19)

17. Comply with a medication regimen as prescribed. (12, 13, 20, 21)

18. Family members or home health service personnel dispense or monitor medications. (22, 23)

19. Increase knowledge of the addictive substance. (4, 24, 25)

20. Keep a daily diary of activities, thoughts, and feelings, as well as mood-altering substance ingestion. (26, 27)

21. Identify specific triggers for substance use. (2, 26, 27, 28)

22. Alter aspects of lifestyle that have become triggers for substance abuse. (29, 31, 32)

23. Substitute positive self-talk for the negative self-talk that mediates the substance abuse behavior. (30)

24. Identify whether anxiety and/or depression serve as underlying states that are self-medicated by substance abuse. (33)

__. _____
   _____
__. _____
   _____
__. _____
   _____

physical illnesses, pain, prescription and OTC medications; alcohol use; nutritional status; cognition, mood and behavior; and social relationships, problems and supports.

11. Assess whether the substance use stems from a long pattern of dependence and/or abuse, or whether the misuse is of relatively recent onset and stems from a specific stressor or mismanagement of a specific medication.

12. Determine whether the medication misuse stems from cognitive inability to self-administer medications appropriately.

13. Work with the patient's physician to determine the safest way to decrease or eliminate physical dependence on the substance(s).

14. Arrange for medical supervision of detoxification if necessary, especially with benzodiazepines.

15. Arrange for a registered dietitian to plan a healthy eating plan, with dietary/vitamin supplementation as necessary.

16. Identify alternative ways of coping with problems other than potentially addictive substances (e.g., a swimming/exercise program for pain rather than analgesics, a widow/widower's group for loneliness rather than alco-

hol, a prescribed sleep regimen rather than sedative/hypnotics, relaxation techniques for tension or pain management rather than anxiolytics).

17. Determine the willingness of the patient to participate in public settings (i.e., AA, group therapy) as an identified user versus more private therapeutic approaches. Refer to AA if willing to attend.

18. Review community resources that are available for older adults with substance use problems (e.g., Alcoholics Anonymous, geropsychiatric hospital units, geriatric detox units, older adult partial hospitalization programs, home health/visiting nurse services, in-home mental health services). Refer to the appropriate level of care.

19. Develop a plan, in conjunction with the patient's physician and, if appropriate, the family, for the patient to control or abstain from substance use.

20. Teach the patient an appropriate medication administration schedule, and how to use pill dispensers available from the pharmacy.

21. Monitor medication compliance by having the patient present the pill dispenser and medication container in

a therapy session; count pills weekly.

22. Teach family members to dispense medications or monitor medication compliance through pill counting.

23. Arrange for medication administration by a family member or home health service if the patient is unable to self-administer appropriately.

24. Assign the patient, and if appropriate the family, reading on the specific substance and its appropriate use and misuse.

25. Identify and assign the patient, and if appropriate the family, to attend community educational events addressing the specific substance.

26. Assign the patient to keep a daily diary of events, places, moods, thoughts, and behaviors, including substance use behaviors.

27. Discuss the diary material with the patient, showing the connections between substance behaviors, moods, thoughts, places, and events.

28. Help the patient to identify specific triggering locations, events, moods, or thoughts for substance use.

29. Discuss the feasibility of changing living arrangements or interpersonal relationships that may be

serving as triggers to substance misuse; assign the patient to make changes as possible.

30. Help the patient to identify and substitute alternative thoughts to substance-triggering cognitions (e.g., instead of "I'll never find another husband like the one I had—I'll have another drink," substitute "I may or may not find another husband, but I can get out and enjoy myself rather than sitting here drinking and feeling sorry for myself.")

31. Direct the patient to substitute new locations (e.g., a movie theater instead of a bar) and new events (e.g., an alcohol-free senior dance instead of a wine and cheese party) in place of substance-triggering locations and events.

32. Ask the patient to make a list of trigger times of day (e.g., cocktail hour, bedtime) and to arrange for an alternate activity (e.g., taking a walk with a friend before dinner, drinking warm milk before bed).

33. Assess for underlying depression and anxiety as triggers for substance misuse. (Consult the Depression and Anxiety chapters of this *Planner* for guidance in treatment, if necessary).

__.   _____
      _____
__.   _____
      _____
__.   _____
      _____

DIAGNOSTIC SUGGESTIONS

Axis I:	303.90	Alcohol Dependence
	305.00	Alcohol Abuse
	304.10	Sedative, Hypnotic, or Anxiolytic Dependence
	305.40	Sedative, Hypnotic, or Anxiolytic Abuse
	305.50	Opioid Abuse
	304.00	Opioid Dependence
	304.80	Polysubstance Dependence
	316	Psychological Factors Affecting Medical Condition
	309.4	Adjustment Disorder with Mixed Disturbance of Emotions and Conduct
	309.9	Adjustment Disorder Unspecified
	_____	_____
	_____	_____

SUICIDAL IDEATION/BEHAVIOR

BEHAVIORAL DEFINITIONS

1. Recurrent thoughts of or preoccupation with taking one's own life.
2. Recurrent thoughts of or preoccupation with a passive wish to die.
3. Persistent or recurring suicidal ideation without any plans.
4. Persistent or recurring suicidal ideation with a specific plan.
5. Recent significant weight loss due to low caloric intake.
6. Refusal to take in enough nutrition and hydration to maintain weight and fluid requirements, when physically and cognitively capable of doing so.
7. Persistent expression of being a burden to the family, hopelessness, having no meaning or purpose in life, having no quality of life, and/or being in constant physical pain.
8. Recent suicide attempt or positive history of suicide attempts.
9. Evidence of access to the means of committing suicide (e.g., weapons, pills).
10. Significant withdrawal from social activities; decline in Activities of Daily Living (ADL) and Instrumental Activities of Daily Living (IADL) functions.

—. _____
   _____
—. _____
   _____
—. _____
   _____

LONG-TERM GOALS

1. Stabilize the suicidal crisis.
2. Alleviate suicidal impulses/ideation.

3. Return to the highest level of previous ADL and IADL functioning.
4. Obtain appropriate pain management.
5. Develop adaptive mechanisms for coping with negative feelings and life events.
6. Resolve issues of feeling like a burden.
7. Reestablish a sense of hopefulness, meaning, and purpose.
8. Develop a satisfying quality of life.

—. _____
   _____
   _____
—. _____
   _____
   _____
—. _____
   _____

SHORT-TERM OBJECTIVES

1. Comply with a suicide prevention procedure of relinquishing potentially dangerous materials such as weapons, hoarded medications, and so forth. (1, 2, 3)

2. Agree to the presence of another person until suicidal threat resolves. (2, 3)

3. Verbalize specific suicidal thoughts, feelings, plans, and actions. (4, 5, 6)

4. Cooperate with psychological testing to assess suicidal risk and depth of depression. (7)

5. Cooperate with a clinical interview to determine the necessity for a more intensive site of service or more intensive services at the current site. (4, 5, 6, 8, 9)

THERAPEUTIC INTERVENTIONS

1. Direct the patient, or instruct the caregiver to direct the patient, to relinquish materials that could be used to commit suicide.

2. Explain to the patient that professional practice laws require that the therapist act to protect the patient from harm from self or others.

3. Stay with the patient, or arrange for a family member or caregiver to stay with the patient, until the danger of imminent harm has passed.

4. Assess the severity of the suicidal ideation by asking the patient to share suicidal history, feelings, thoughts, plans, and behaviors.

6. Agree to the level of care necessary to protect from suicidal impulses; understand that if danger to self persists, involuntary care will be pursued. (8, 9, 10, 11)

7. Comply with a psychopharmacological medication regimen as prescribed. (12, 13)

8. Report effect/side-effect information accurately to the therapist and to the prescribing physician. (13, 14)

9. Verbalize a promise to contact a therapist, family member, physician, or religious counselor if a serious urge toward self-harm arises. (15, 16, 17)

10. Verbalize feelings of guilt; being a burden; hopelessness; helplessness; having no meaning or purpose; and/or being angry at self, family, or God. (4, 15, 18, 19)

11. Identify the thoughts and situation appraisals associated with negative feelings. (20)

12. Identify the thoughts and situation appraisals that are based on irrational beliefs. (21)

13. Challenge and replace irrational beliefs with more positive, hopeful self-talk. (21, 22, 23)

14. List multiple alternate ways of coping with realistically negative situations. (24, 25)

15. List the consequences of each potential solution of

5. Distinguish carefully between thoughts of death that are age-appropriate, wishing to die that may be disease state–specific and appropriate, and suicidal ideation and maybe a sign of underlying depression that requires treatment.

6. Assess whether the suicidal ideation/behavior is active (e.g., involves guns, medications, or plastic bags) or passive (e.g., involves refusing food, fluid, or therapeutic treatments).

7. Arrange for administration of the Geriatric Depression Scale, the CES-D, Modified Scale for Suicidal Ideation, or other objective assessment instruments. Evaluate the results and give feedback to the patient.

8. Arrange for transfer of the patient to a more intensive care site (e.g., geropsychiatric inpatient unit or day hospital).

9. Arrange for more intensive treatment services at the current site (e.g., one-on-one supervision, antidepressant medication, daily psychotherapy).

10. Help the patient understand that passive suicidal ideation/behavior results in death and often signals treatable underlying depression or pain.

coping with negative situations. (26)

16. Choose a method of coping with a negative situation that comes the closest to a desirable solution while minimizing negative outcomes for self and others. (27)

17. Develop an action plan to carry out the chosen method of coping. (28, 29)

18. Identify primary people in the support network. (30)

19. Verbalize an assessment of the ability of the current support network to help meet the needs for support. (31, 32, 33, 34)

20. Explore avenues for building additional support (disease-specific support groups, faith-based groups, widowhood groups, senior support groups). (34, 35)

21. Make appropriate, direct requests for help from family, friends, and the wider support network. (33, 35, 36, 37)

22. Verbalize appreciation for the empathy and support of the staff, family, and friends. (38)

23. Express the burden of experiencing chronic pain. (18, 19, 39)

24. Comply with a pain management evaluation. (40, 41, 42)

25. Comply with a pain management program as prescribed. (42)

11. Review the patient's advance directives and medical condition/prognosis with the attending physician; evaluate whether treatment refusal is consistent with advance directives and current condition; rule out treatable conditions such as depression and pain.

12. Instill hope in the patient that help and support is forthcoming, that problems can be solved, that burdens of pain and psychological suffering can be reduced if the patient will cooperate with the care.

13. Arrange for a physician to examine the patient to assess suicidal ideation/behavior, order medications as indicated, titrate medications, and monitor for side effects.

14. Encourage compliance with medications and help with recording of effects/side effects so that the patient can communicate effectively with the prescribing physician.

15. Explain to the patient the importance of sharing suicidal thoughts and feelings with others so that help can be arranged. Solicit a promise to report serious suicidal urges to caregivers.

16. Help all care team members (patient, family, physician, therapist, caregivers, etc.)

26. Identify sources of pleasure, hope, and meaning. (43)

27. Construct a daily schedule that includes at least one pleasurable, future-oriented, and/or meaningful activity each day. (44, 45)

28. Practice a healthy lifestyle, and continue building problem-solving skills and a social support network to prevent future suicidal episodes. (46, 47)

___. _____

_____

___. _____

_____

___. _____

_____

understand the need to take verbal and behavioral expressions of suicidal ideation/behavior seriously.

17. Help the care team members develop an action plan with designated responsible persons to provide intense supervision of the patient if suicidal ideation/behavior should recur.

18. Explore the negative feelings (guilt, anger, hopelessness, helplessness) that led the patient to consider suicide as a solution.

19. Assist the patient with the release of negative feelings through expressions of anger, hopelessness, grief, and shame; provide comfort and security while the patient ventilates feelings.

20. Help the patient explore and identify specific thoughts and appraisals (I believe I am a burden; I can no longer stand this pain; life isn't worth living without my spouse) that are associated with the negative feelings.

21. Help the patient identify which beliefs are distorted, irrational, or unnecessarily pessimistic; provide examples of alternate, constructive, and/or optimistic cognitive interpretations.

22. Review each original negative belief with the patient and identify alternate positive ways of thinking about

or appraising the situation; have the patient write an alternate, more potentially constructive belief next to each negative belief.

23. Help the patient understand that faulty reasoning, poor problem-solving skills, an inadequate support network, and/or untreated depression or pain can lead to suicidal ideation/behavior.

24. Teach the patient to brainstorm alternate solutions to problems, rather than focusing narrowly on a single pessimistic or no solution.

25. Assist the patient with accepting that approximate solutions to problems can be satisfying even if perfect solutions cannot be found.

26. Teach the patient the problem-solving process of forecasting objective and subjective consequences for self and others of each potential solution; have the patient write down all potential solutions and consequences.

27. Assist the patient with the decision-making process to maximize positive outcomes and minimize negative outcomes; remind the patient that less than perfect solutions to problems can still be satisfying.

28. Discuss with the patient the actual steps he/she would need to take, or ask others to take, that would begin

the problem resolution process.

29. Encourage the patient to make the assertive statements and/or take the assertive actions necessary to move toward problem resolution.

30. Instruct the patient to list all family members, friends, religious counselors, caregivers, physicians, and others who have or could provide emotional or moral support.

31. Instruct the patient to list all the areas in which support is currently, or is anticipated to be, necessary: daily function, psychological, spiritual, legal, medical, financial, and so forth.

32. Review with the patient the list of people in the support network, their abilities and time availability, and the patient's comfort level in asking them for help.

33. Assist the patient in determining what specific help to ask for and from which members of the support network.

34. Help the patient to identify needs that remain unmet by the current support system.

35. Refer the patient to aging services to obtain additional support, such as the Area Agency on Aging, faith-based aging services, pri-

vate geriatric care management, or other community services as available.

36. Discuss with the patient the right and the responsibility to ask for help directly and assertively, rather than through indirect means such as suicide.

37. Develop an action plan with time frames for the patient to arrange for needs to be met. Reinforce assertiveness.

38. Encourage the patient to verbalize appreciation to members of the support network and to reciprocate as able.

39. Assist the patient with the ventilation of feelings regarding chronic pain.

40. Teach the patient to keep a pain diary to heighten awareness of the relationship of pain to time of day, medication administration, events, people, places, activities, thoughts, and feelings.

41. Refer the patient to a pain management program for a full evaluation.

42. With the patient's consent, request a verbal or written report from the pain clinic to encourage his/her compliance with the pain management program.

43. As immediate problems begin to resolve, help the patient to build positive prevention structures into

life through the identification of sources of pleasure, hope, and meaning; have the patient list current and potential sources.

44. Assign the patient to fill out a week's schedule with at least one pleasurable (e.g., going to a music concert with a friend), future-oriented (working on a needlecraft graduation present for a grandchild, planting seeds), and/or meaningful (e.g., volunteering to read books at a child-care center) activity each day.

45. Review satisfaction with the week's activities with the patient, adjust as necessary, and continue to encourage the process.

46. Encourage the patient to join community groups and activities that support a physically and psychologically healthy lifestyle.

47. Monitor continued ability to apply new concepts learned in cognitive restructuring, problem solving, and use of social support; adjust, reinforce, and reteach as necessary.

__. _____

_____

__. _____

_____

__. _____

_____

DIAGNOSTIC SUGGESTIONS

Axis I:	291.8	Alcohol-Induced Mood Disorder
	292.84	Sedative-, Hypnotic-, or Anxiolytic-Induced Mood Disorder
	296.xx	Major Depressive Disorder
	300.4	Dysthymic Disorder
	296.xx	Bipolar I Disorder
	296.89	Bipolar II Disorder
	293.83	Mood Disorder Due to (Axis III Disorder)
	307.89	Pain Disorder Associated with Both Psychological Factors and a General Medical Condition
	309.xx	Adjustment Disorder
	316	Psychological Factors Affecting Medical Condition
	995.2	Adverse Effects of Medication NOS
	_____	_____
	_____	_____

WANDERING/WAY-FINDING DEFICIT

BEHAVIORAL DEFINITIONS

1. Getting lost while attempting to reach a formerly familiar location (e.g., grocery store).
2. Reporting periods of confusion when driving.
3. Reporting perception of unfamiliarity when in formerly familiar places.
4. Unable to follow navigational directions, either in a car or on foot.
5. Unable to learn new pathways (e.g., getting from the bedroom to the dining room in a new residence).
6. Being in an inappropriate or unsafe location without rationale (e.g., on the street in the middle of the night).
7. Leaving a supervised area without being able to verbalize a rational destination point.
8. Constantly attempting to leave a supervised area.

—. _____
   _____
—. _____
   _____
—. _____
   _____

LONG-TERM GOALS

1. Improve personal safety and that of others.
2. Improve spatial functioning through the use of compensatory strategies.

3. Decrease the wandering/way-finding deficit by resolving causative factors related to medication side effects, anxiety, and/or treatable medical conditions.
4. Accept and understand the extent of and causes for the wandering/way-finding deficits.
5. Accept and adjust to a decreased opportunity for mobility.
6. Accept and adjust to the possible need for an increased level of personal and/or electronic supervision.

—. _____

_____

—. _____

_____

—. _____

_____

SHORT-TERM OBJECTIVES

1. Consent to participate in an evaluation of a wandering/way-finding disorder if decisionally capable; surrogate consents if the patient is not decisionally capable. (1)

2. Cooperate with an evaluation to identify the specific behavioral pattern of wandering or way-finding difficulties. (2, 3)

3. Cooperate with an evaluation to identify medical, neuropsychological, or psychological causative factors of behavior. (4, 5, 6)

4. Participate in an evaluation of driving capability. (7)

5. Verbalize an understanding and acceptance of causes for and extent of driving/way-finding deficit. (8, 9)

THERAPEUTIC INTERVENTIONS

1. Obtain consent from the patient or surrogate to address the problem of wandering/way-finding deficit.

2. Conduct a behavioral analysis through direct observation, patient report, and/or proxy report (family or staff); detail frequency of episodes, time of day, location, precipitants, and consequences, observed/reported mood and rationale, and response to suggestions for change.

3. Evaluate the severity of danger to self and others based on the preceding data; take immediate action as necessary to prevent harm to self or others.

6. Comply with a physician's recommendations to treat reversible causes of driving/way-finding deficit. (10)

7. Take additional preparation time before traveling alone to review and write down the destination and route. (11)

8. Determine the relative effectiveness of narrative and visual direction aids; seek out and use a more effective method. (12)

9. Limit driving to familiar destinations, a safe radius from home, the safest times of day, and the safest roads. (13)

10. Drive with passengers who do not experience spatial confusion. (14, 15)

11. Participate in a driver's refresher course for seniors. (16)

12. Participate in ongoing monitoring of the driving/way-finding deficit. (17)

13. Agree to relinquish driver's license if the deficit cannot be reversed or compensated for. (18, 19, 20)

14. Verbalize feelings of loss, sadness, anger, embarrassment, fear of future decline, and impotence that may accompany the loss of ability to drive. (21)

15. Learn alternative strategies for maintaining mobility and activity when no longer driving. (22, 23)

4. Refer to the physician for an evaluation of prescribed and OTC medications and medical conditions that could be causing confusion or spatial disorientation.

5. Conduct or refer for a neuropsychological evaluation to determine if confusion/spatial disorientation is an isolated phenomenon or part of a larger problem of cognitive decline.

6. Conduct or refer for a psychological evaluation to assess the possible contributions of depression and/or anxiety to a wandering/way-finding deficit.

7. Refer to a driver evaluation program (e.g., at a rehabilitation hospital or state driver's examination).

8. Integrate and feed back findings of all evaluations with the patient, physician, and family members as appropriate.

9. Meet with the patient individually to process reaction to feedback until he/she is able to understand and accept the cause(s) and significance of a driving/way-finding deficit.

10. Discuss a change in medication regimen and plans for further medical workup from the physician; reinforce the new regimen and compliance with further medical evaluation with the patient and family as appropriate.

16. Verbalize satisfaction with increased safety for self and others. (24)

17. Navigate independently within own residence. (25, 26, 27)

18. Decrease or eliminate attempts to exit the residence without a rational destination point. (28, 29, 30, 31, 32, 33)

19. Decrease or eliminate unsupervised exiting from the residence. (34, 35)

20. Decrease or eliminate episodes of being lost. (36)

21. Increase safety if lost episode does occur. (37)

—. _____
_____

—. _____
_____

—. _____
_____

11. Assign the patient to spend five minutes preparing for each trip alone outside the home; direct the patient to review and write down the destination and route.

12. Teach the patient to use both narrative guides (e.g., turn left at the second light) and maps to find a route; have the patient experiment with both, report back on, and use the most effective method.

13. Review with the patient, and family if appropriate, current use of a car. Develop a plan to eliminate unnecessary trips; find substitute transportation where possible; limit driving to specified times of the day (e.g., not after dark, not during rush hour), to a specified radius from home, to familiar destinations, and to specified roads (e.g., secondary roads only, no highways).

14. Assign the patient the task of identifying friends, acquaintances, or volunteers from senior agencies or religious organizations who have no difficulty with way-finding.

15. Direct the patient to request that individuals without way-finding deficits accompany them on trips.

16. Direct the patient to investigate the offerings of senior refresher courses in driving

(e.g., the *55 Alive* course offered by AARP); encourage the patient to take the course.

17. Repeat behavioral analysis of way-finding deficit episodes described in number 2 to monitor the effectiveness of interventions in reducing frequency or severity.

18. Gather all data on episodes, evaluations, interventions, and postintervention monitoring; evaluate the extent of continuing danger to self or others based on the data.

19. Discuss the results with the patient, physician, and if appropriate, family member; determine who should request that the patient relinquish his/her driver's license if necessary.

20. Meet with the patient individually or with the family; gently confront with evidence of danger to self or others, and request that his/her license be relinquished.

21. Encourage the patient to express feelings about the loss of his/her license as a first step toward adaptation.

22. As anger and grief wane, introduce a problem-solving discussion about alternative modes of transportation.

23. If no transportation can be secured to old activities,

help the patient identify
alternative activities to
maintain an active and
engaged lifestyle.

24. Praise the patient for being
a prosocial and responsible
member of the community;
encourage him/her to
become an advocate for road
safety and a counselor to
peers who are in a driving
transition period.

25. Arrange for caregivers
(family or staff) to place
signs (verbal and pictorial)
within the residence that
label rooms (e.g., a picture
of a toilet on the bathroom)
and that give directions to
key areas (e.g., "to dining
room").

26. Teach caregivers to color-
code rooms for different
functions (e.g., in congre-
gate residence, different
individuals have different
color rooms and decora-
tions, including exterior
doorjamb color).

27. Teach caregivers to post
framed function-associated
material on the walls outside the doors (e.g., personal
picture and objects outside
the bedroom; knife, plate,
and fork outside the dining
room, etc.).

28. Using behavioral analysis, a
discussion with the individual, and trial and error,
work with caregivers to
determine the cause of the
exit-seeking behavior: phys-

ical discomfort, anxiety, boredom, need for physical activity, loneliness, or other cause.

29. If exit-seeking is triggered by physical needs, teach the caregivers to provide food or fluid; check need for the bathroom; or provide with a pain reliever.

30. If exit seeking is triggered by anxiety, teach the caregivers to provide reassurance, give the individual an opportunity to reminisce about home and family; distract him/her with a job or task; listen to a tape-recorded reassurance message.

31. If exit seeking is triggered by boredom, teach the caregivers to involve the individual in a simple tactile activity, such as folding socks or towels or winding yarn.

32. If exit seeking is triggered by a need for physical activity, teach the caregivers to find an enclosed, safe but interesting space for the individual to walk.

33. If exit seeking is triggered by loneliness, teach the caregivers to walk with the individual, holding hands if it helps, or to engage the individual with another person or a group.

34. Teach the caregivers to attach a red velcro strip across the exit, hang red

streamers in front of the door, or place a bold red "STOP!" sign on the exit door.

35. Assign caregivers the task of investigating and selecting an electronic surveillance method, such as WanderGuard, that alerts caregivers when the individual is leaving the premises.

36. Educate the caregivers about the need for continual supervision, and decide on and arrange for a physical and interpersonal milieu that can meet the need.

37. Assign the caregivers the task of investigating and selecting safety identification items such as Medic-Alert bracelets, which will instantly identify an individual who is lost and give a contact name and number.

__. _____
   _____
__. _____
   _____
__. _____
   _____

DIAGNOSTIC SUGGESTIONS

Axis I:

293.0	Delirium Due to (Axis III Disorder)
291.0	Alcohol Intoxication or Withdrawal Delirium
292.0	Sedative, Hypnotic, or Anxiolytic Withdrawal
292.81	Other or Unknown Substance-Induced Delirium
290.xx	Dementia of the Alzheimer's Type or Vascular Dementia
294.1	Dementia Due to (Head Trauma, Parkinson's Disease, Huntington's Disease, or Axis III Disorder)
290.10	Dementia Due to Pick's Disease or Creutzfeldt-Jakob Disease
294.8	Dementia NOS
291.2	Alcohol-Induced Persisting Dementia
294.0	Amnestic Disorder Due to (Axis III Disorder)
291.1	Alcohol-Induced Persisting Amnestic Disorder
294.8	Amnestic Disorder NOS
294.9	Cognitive Disorder NOS
995.2	Adverse Effects of Medication NOS
780.9	Age-Related Cognitive Decline
316	Psychological Factors Affecting Medical Condition
_____	_____
_____	_____

Appendix A

BIBLIOTHERAPY SUGGESTIONS

Activities of Daily Living/Instrumental Activities of Daily Living Deficits

Cleveland, J. (1998). *Simplifying Life as a Senior Citizen*. New York: St. Martin's Griffin

Mace, N. L., and P. V. Rabins. (1991). *The Thirty-Six-Hour Day: A Family Guide to Caring for Persons with Alzheimer's Disease, Related Dementing Illnesses, and Memory Loss in Later Life*. Baltimore, MD: Johns Hopkins.

Aggression (Verbal and/or Physical)

Bower, S. A., and G. H. Bower. (1991). *Asserting Yourself: A Practical Guide for Positive Change*. Reading, MA: Addison-Wesley.

Gruetzner, H. (1997). *Alzheimer's: A Complete Guide for Families and Loved Ones*. New York: John Wiley & Sons.

Hussian, R. A., and R. L. Davis. (1985). *Responsive Care: Behavioral Interventions with Elderly Persons*. Champaign, IL: Research Press.

Kaplan, M., and S. B. Hoffman. (1998). *Behaviors in Dementia: Best Practices for Successful Management*. Baltimore, MD: Health Professions Press.

Anxiety

Benson, H. (1975). *The Relaxation Response*. New York: William Morrow.

Davis, M., E. Eshelman, and M. McKay. (1988). *The Relaxation and Stress Reduction Workbook*. Oakland, CA: New Harbinger.

Fossum, L. (1990). *Overcoming Anxiety: A Primer for Better Life Management*. Menlo Park, CA: Crisp Publications.

Hauck, P. (1975). *Overcoming Worry and Fear*. Philadelphia, PA: Westminster Press.

Caregiver Distress

Berman, C. (1996). *Caring for Yourself While Caring for Your Aging Parents: How to Help, How to Survive.* New York: Henry Holt.

Cohen, D., and C. Eisdorfer. (1993). *Caring for Your Aging Parents: A Planning and Action Guide.* New York: Penguin Putnam.

Lee, A. J., and M. Callender. (1998). *The Complete Guide to Eldercare.* Hauppauge, NY: Barron's.

Loverde, J. (1997). *The Complete Eldercare Planner: Where to Start, Questions to Ask, and How to Find Help.* New York: Hyperion.

Communication Deficits

Dugan, M. B. (1997). *Keys to Living with Hearing Loss.* Hauppauge, NY: Barron's.

Feil, N. (1993). *The Validation Breakthrough: Simple Techniques for Communicating with People with Alzheimer's-Type Dementia.* Baltimore, MD: Health Professions Press.

Pietro, M. J. S., and E. Ostuni. (1997). *Successful Communications with Alzheimer's Disease Patients: An In-Service Training Manual.* Boston: Butterworth-Heinemann.

Turkington, C.A. (1997). *The Hearing Loss Sourcebook: A Complete Guide to Coping with Hearing Loss and Where to Get Help.* New York: Plume.

Decision-Making Capacity Unresolved

Nelson, J. L., and H. L. Nelson. (1997). *Alzheimer's: Answers to Hard Questions for Families.* New York: Main Street Books.

Strauss, P. J., and N. M. Lederman. (1996). *The Elder Law Handbook: A Legal and Financial Survival Guide for Caregivers and Seniors.* New York: Facts on File.

Depression

Burns, D. (1989). *The Feeling Good Handbook.* New York: Plume Penguin.

Carter, L., and F. Minirth. (1995). *The Freedom from Depression Workbook.* Nashville, TN: Thomas Nelson.

Frankl, V. (1992). *Man's Search for Meaning: An Introduction to Logotherapy.* Boston: Beacon.

Greenberger, D., and C. Padesky. (1995). *Mind over Mood: Change How You Feel by Changing the Way You Think.* New York: Guilford.

Lewinsohn, P. M., R. F. Munoz, M. A. Youngren, and A. Zeiss. (1992). *Control Your Depression.* New York: Fireside Simon & Schuster.

Simon, J. (1993). *Good Mood: The New Psychology of Overcoming Depression.* LaSalle, IL: Open Court.

Grief/Loss Unresolved

Byock, I. (1997). *Dying Well: Peace and Possibilities at the End of Life.* New York: Riverhead.

Deits, B. (1992). *Life after Loss: A Personal Guide Dealing with Death, Divorce, Job Change and Relocation.* Tucson, AZ: Fisher.

Kok, J. (1997). *Waiting for Morning: Finding God in Human Suffering.* Grand Rapids, MI: CRC Publications.

Kubler-Ross, E. (1969). *On Death and Dying.* New York: Touchstone Simon & Schuster.

Kushner, H. (1981). *When Bad Things Happen to Good People.* New York: Schocken Books.

Rando, T. (1991). *How to Go On Living When Someone You Love Dies.* New York: Bantam.

Zonnebelt-Smeenge, S., and R. DeVries. (1998). *Getting to the Other Side of Grief: Overcoming the Loss of a Spouse.* Grand Rapids, MI: Baker Books.

Interpersonal Conflict

Bach, G., and P. Wyden. (1976). *The Intimate Enemy: How to Fight Fair in Love and Marriage.* New York: Avon.

Fromm, E. (1956). *The Art of Loving.* New York: Harper & Row.

Jandt, F. (1985). *Win-Win Negotiating: Turning Conflict into Agreement.* New York: John Wiley & Sons.

Nissenboim, S., and C. Vroman. (1998). *The Positive Interactions Program of Activities for People with Alzheimer's Disease.* Baltimore, MD: Health Professions Press.

Life Role Transition

Birren, J. E., and L. Feldman. (1997). *Where to Go from Here: Discovering Your Own Life's Wisdom in the Second Half of Your Life.* New York: Simon & Schuster.

Butler, R. N., and M. I. Lewis. (1993). *Love and Sex after 60.* New York: Ballantine.

Erikson, E. H., J. M. Erikson, and H. O. Kivnick. (1986). *Vital Involvement in Old Age.* New York: W. W. Norton.

Johnson, E., and K. McFadden. (1997). *Senior Net's Official Guide to the Web: A Complete Cyberguide to the Web for People over 55!* Emeryville, CA: Lycos.

Rowe, J. W., and R. L. Kahn. (1998). *Successful Aging.* New York: Pantheon.
Skinner, B. F., and M. E. Vaughan. (1997). *Enjoy Old Age: A Practical Guide.* New York: W. W. Norton.

Loneliness/Interpersonal Deficit

Burns, D. (1985). *Intimate Connections: The New Clinically Tested Program for Overcoming Loneliness.* New York: William Morrow.
Zimbardo, P. (1987). *Shyness: What It Is and What to Do About It.* Reading, MA: Addison-Wesley.

Mania/Hypomania

Copeland, M. E. (1994). *Living without Depression and Manic Depression: A Workbook for Maintaining Mood Stability.* Oakland, CA: New Harbinger.
Duke, P., and G. Hochman. (1993). *A Brilliant Madness: Living with Manic-Depressive Illness.* New York: Bantam.
Jamison, K. R. (1997). *An Unquiet Mind.* New York: Random House.

Medical/Medication Issues Unresolved

Hayflick, L. (1996). *How and Why We Age.* New York: Ballantine.
Swedo, S., and H. Leonard. (1996). *It's Not All in Your Head: The Real Causes of and Newest Solutions for Women's Most Common Health Problems.* San Francisco: HarperCollins.
Williams, M. (1995). *The American Geriatrics Society Complete Guide to Aging and Health.* New York: Harmony.

Memory Impairment

Baddeley, A. (1996). *Your Memory: A User's Guide.* London: Prion.
Howard, P. J. (1994). *The Owner's Manual for the Brain: Everyday Applications from Mind-Brain Research.* Austin, TX: Bard.
Lapp, D. C. (1995). *Don't Forget! Easy Exercises for a Better Memory.* Reading, MA: Addison-Wesley.
Stern, L., and J. Fogler. (1998). *Improving Your Memory: A Guide for Older Adults.* Ann Arbor, MI: Memory Skills.

Nutritional Deficits Unresolved

Fries, J. F. (1998). *Living Well: Taking Care of Your Health in the Middle and Later Years.* Reading, MA: Addison-Wesley.

Murphy, J. (1991). *Keys to Nutrition over Fifty*. Hauppage, NY: Barron's.

Oliver, M. (1989). *Margo Oliver's Cookbook for Seniors: Nutritious Recipes for One-Two-or More*. Bellingham, WA: Self Counsel Press.

Obsessive-Compulsive Behaviors

Baer, L. (1992). *Getting Control: Overcoming Your Obsessions and Compulsions*. New York: Penguin.

Foa, E., and R. Wilson. (1991). *S.T.O.P. Obsessing: How to Overcome Your Obsessions and Compulsions*. New York: Bantam.

Steketee, G., and K. White. (1990). *When Once Is Not Enough: Help for Obsessive Compulsives*. Oakland, CA: New Harbinger.

Paranoid Ideation

Cohl, H. A. (1997). *Are We Scaring Ourselves to Death?: How Pessimism, Paranoia, and a Misguided Media Are Leading Us toward Disaster*. New York: St. Martin's Press.

Ross, J. (1994). *Triumph over Fear*. New York: Bantam Books.

Phobia/Panic/Agoraphobia

Babior, S., and C. Goldman. (1996). *Overcoming Panic, Anxiety and Phobias: New Strategies to Free Yourself from Worry and Fear*. Duluth, MN: Whole Person Associates.

Swede, S., and S. Jaffe. (1987). *The Panic Attack Recovery Book*. New York: New American Library.

Physical/Sexual/Financial Abuse Victim

American Bar Association. (1998). *Legal Guide for Older Americans: The Law Every American Over Fifty Needs to Know*. New York: Random House.

Camille, P. (1996). *Getting Older, Getting Fleeced: The National Shame of Financial Elder Abuse and How to Avoid It*. Santa Barbara, CA: Fithian Press.

Pillemer, K. A., and R. S. Wolf. (1993). *Elder Abuse: Conflict in the Family*. Westport, CT: Auburn House.

Quinn, M. J., and S. K. Tomita. (1997). *Elder Abuse and Neglect: Causes, Diagnosis, and Intervention Strategies*. New York: Springer.

Residential Issues Unresolved

Brawley, E. C. (1997). *Designing for Alzheimer's Disease: Strategies for Creating Better Care Environments*. New York: John Wiley & Sons.

Cleveland, J. (1996). *Everything You Need to Know about Retirement Housing: Finding the Right Place at the Right Time.* New York: Penguin.

Warner, M. L. (1998). *The Complete Guide to Alzheimer's Proofing Your Home.* West Lafayette, IN: Purdue University Press.

Sexually Inappropriate/Disinhibited Behavior

Davidson, F. G. (1996). *The Alzheimer's Sourcebook for Caregivers: A Practical Guide for Getting through the Day.* Los Angeles: Lowell House.

Hellen, C. R. (1992). *Alzheimer's Disease: Activity-Focused Care.* Boston: Butterworth-Heinemann.

Sleep Disturbance

Dotto, L. (1990). *Losing Sleep: How Your Sleeping Habits Affect Your Life.* New York: William Morrow.

Lewis, C. B., and L. C. Campanelli. (1990). *Health Promotion and Exercise for Older Adults: An Instructor's Guide.* New York: Aspen.

Maas, J., M. L. Wherry, B. R. Hogan, and J. Blumen. (1998). *Power Sleep: The Revolutionary Program That Prepares Your Mind for Peak Performance.* New York: Villard.

Somatization

Benson, H. (1980). *The Mind-Body Effect.* New York: Simon & Schuster.

Jahnke, R. (1997). *The Healer Within: The Four Essential Self-Care Techniques for Optimal Health.* San Francisco: HarperCollins.

Kabat-Zinn, J. (1990). *Full Catastrophe Living: Using the Wisdom of Your Body and Mind to Face Stress, Pain, and Illness.* New York: Delta.

Spiritual Confusion

May, R. (1953). *Man's Search for Himself.* New York: W. W. Norton.

McKim, D. K. (1998). *God Never Forgets: Faith, Hope and Alzheimer's Disease.* Louisville, KY: Westminster John Knox Press.

Substance Dependence/Misuse

Graham, K., et al. (1995). *Addictions Treatment for Older Adults.* Binghamton, NY: Haworth.

Ruben, D. H. (1990). *The Aging and Drug Effects: A Planning Manual for Medication and Alcohol Abuse Treatment of the Elderly.* Jefferson, NC: McFarland & Company.

Tate, P. (1996). *Alcohol: How to Give It Up and Be Glad You Did*. San Francisco: See Sharp Press.

Vandeputte, C. (1991). *Alcohol, Medications, and Older Adults: A Guide for Families and Other Caregivers*. Minneapolis, MN: Johnson Institute.

West, J. W., and B. Ford. (1997). *The Betty Ford Center Book of Answers: Help for Those Struggling with Substance Abuse and for the People Who Love Them*. New York: Pocket Books.

Suicidal Ideation/Behavior

Clark, N. (1997). *The Politics of Physician Assisted Suicide*. New York: Garland.

Kok, J. (1997). *Waiting for Morning: Finding God in Human Suffering*. Grand Rapids, MI: CRC Publications.

Lester, D., and M. Tallmer. (1993). *Now I Lay Me Down: Suicide in the Elderly*. Philadelphia: The Charles Press.

Richman, J. (1993). *Preventing Elderly Suicide: Overcoming Personal Despair, Professional Neglect, and Social Bias*. New York: Springer.

Seligman, M. (1990). *Learned Optimism: The Skill to Conquer Life's Obstacles, Large and Small*. New York: Pocket Books.

Wandering/Way-Finding Deficit

Dowling, J. R., and N. L. Mace. (1995). *Keeping Busy: A Handbook of Activities for Persons with Dementia*. Baltimore: Johns Hopkins.

Rader, J., and E. M. Tornquist. (1995). *Individualized Dementia Care: Creative, Compassionate Approaches*. New York: Springer.

Appendix B

INDEX OF DSM-IV CODES ASSOCIATED WITH PRESENTING PROBLEMS

Acute Stress Disorder   308.3
  Anxiety
  Grief/Loss Unresolved
  Interpersonal Conflict
  Life Role Transition
  Loneliness/Interpersonal Deficits
  Physical/Sexual/Financial Abuse
  Residential Issues Unresolved

Adjustment Disorder   309.xx
  ADL/IADL Deficits
  Aggression/Hostility
  Caregiver Distress
  Communication Deficits
  Depression
  Grief/Loss Unresolved
  Interpersonal Conflict
  Life Role Transition
  Loneliness/Interpersonal Deficits
  Nutritional Deficits Unresolved
  Physical/Sexual/Financial Abuse
  Residential Issues Unresolved
  Spiritual Confusion
  Suicidal Ideation/Behavior

Adjustment Disorders with Disturbance of Conduct   309.3
  Sexually Inappropriate/Disinhibited
    Behavior

Adjustment Disorder with Mixed Disturbance of Emotions and Conduct   309.4
  Substance Dependence/Misuse

Adjustment Disorder Unspecified   309.9
  Substance Dependence/Misuse

Adverse Effects of Medication NOS   995.2
  ADL/IADL Deficits
  Aggression/Hostility
  Communication Deficits
  Decisional Incapacity
  Depression
  Medical/Medication Issues
  Memory Impairment
  Nutritional Deficits Unresolved
  Paranoid Ideation
  Sexually Inappropriate/Disinhibited
    Behavior
  Spiritual Confusion
  Suicidal Ideation/Behavior
  Wandering/Way-Finding Deficit

Age-Related Cognitive Decline   780.9
  Memory Impairment
  Wandering/Way-Finding Deficit

Agoraphobia without History of Panic Disorder   300.22
  Anxiety
  Phobia/Panic/Agoraphobia

Alcohol Abuse   305.00
  Substance Dependence/Misuse

Alcohol Dependence   303.90
Obsessive-Compulsive Disorder
Substance Dependence/Misuse

**Alcohol-Induced Mood
Disorder**   291.8
Suicidal Ideation/Behavior

**Alcohol-Induced Persisting
Amnestic Disorder**   291.1
Memory Impairment
Wandering/Way-Finding Deficit

**Alcohol-Induced Persisting
Dementia**   291.2
ADL/IADL Deficits
Aggression/Hostility
Communication Deficits
Decisional Incapacity
Memory Impairment
Sexually Inappropriate/Disinhibited
  Behavior
Wandering/Way-Finding Deficit

**Alcohol-Induced Sleep
Disorder**   291.8
Sleep Disturbance

**Alcohol Intoxication
or Withdrawal Delirium**   291.0
Memory Impairment
Sexually Inappropriate/Disinhibited
  Behavior
Wandering/Way-Finding Deficit

**Amnestic Disorder Due to
[Axis III Disorder]**   294.0
Memory Impairment
Wandering/Way-Finding Deficit

Amnestic Disorder NOS   294.8
Memory Impairment
Wandering/Way-Finding Deficit

**Anxiety Disorder Due to
[Axis III Disorder]**   293.89
ADL/IADL Deficits
Aggression/Hostility
Anxiety
Communication Deficits

Decisional Incapacity
Medical/Medication Issues
Sexually Inappropriate/Disinhibited
  Behavior
Somatization

Anxiety Disorder NOS   300.00
ADL/IADL Deficits
Aggression/Hostility
Anxiety
Caregiver Distress
Communication Deficits
Depression
Grief/Loss Unresolved
Interpersonal Conflict
Life Role Transition
Loneliness/Interpersonal Deficits
Medical/Medication Issues
Nutritional Deficits Unresolved
Obsessive-Compulsive Disorder
Sexually Inappropriate/Disinhibited
  Behavior
Spiritual Confusion

Bipolar I Disorder   296.xx
Decisional Incapacity
Depression
Mania/Hypomania
Suicidal Ideation/Behavior

Bipolar II Disorder   296.89
Decisional Incapacity
Depression
Mania/Hypomania
Suicidal Ideation/Behavior

Bipolar Disorder NOS   296.80
Mania/Hypomania

**Breathing-Related Sleep
Disorder**   780.59
Sleep Disturbance

Brief Psychotic Disorder   298.8
Physical/Sexual/Financial Abuse

**Circadian Rhythm Sleep
Disorder**   307.45
Sleep Disturbance

Cognitive Disorder NOS   294.9
ADL/IADL Deficits
Aggression/Hostility

Dysthymic Disorder　　　300.4
　Caregiver Distress
　Depression
　Grief/Loss Unresolved
　Interpersonal Conflict
　Life Role Transition
　Loneliness/Interpersonal Deficits
　Medical/Medication Issues
　Nutritional Deficits Unresolved
　Physical/Sexual/Financial Abuse
　Residential Issues Unresolved
　Spiritual Confusion
　Suicidal Ideation/Behavior

**Generalized Anxiety
Disorder**　　　300.02
　ADL/IADL Deficits
　Aggression/Hostility
　Anxiety
　Caregiver Distress
　Communication Deficits
　Depression
　Medical/Medication Issues
　Nutritional Deficits Unresolved
　Physical/Sexual/Financial Abuse
　Residential Issues Unresolved
　Sexually Inappropriate/Disinhibited
　　Behavior
　Somatization
　Spiritual Confusion

Hypochondriasis　　　300.7
　Somatization

**Insomnia Related to . . . [*Axis I
or Axis II Disorder*]**　　　307.42
　Sleep Disturbance

Major Depressive Disorder　296.xx
　ADL/IADL Deficits
　Aggression/Hostility
　Caregiver Distress
　Decisional Incapacity
　Depression
　Grief/Loss Unresolved
　Interpersonal Conflict
　Life Role Transition
　Loneliness/Interpersonal Deficits
　Medical/Medication Issues
　Nutritional Deficits Unresolved
　Obsessive-Compulsive Disorder
　Physical/Sexual/Financial Abuse

　Residential Issues Unresolved
　Sexually Inappropriate/Disinhibited
　　Behavior
　Spiritual Confusion
　Suicidal Ideation/Behavior

**Mental Disorder NOS Due to
an Axis III Disorder**　　　293.9
　Decisional Incapacity
　Medical/Medication Issues
　Physical/Sexual/Financial Abuse
　Residential Issues Unresolved

**Mood Disorder Due to
[*Axis III Disorder*]**　　　293.83
　Suicidal Ideation/Behavior

**Obsessive-Compulsive
Disorder**　　　300.3
　Anxiety
　Obsessive-Compulsive Disorder

Opioid Abuse　　　305.50
　Substance Dependence/Misuse

Opioid Dependence　　　304.00
　Substance Dependence/Misuse

**Other or Unknown Substance-
Induced Delirium**　　　292.81
　Memory Impairment
　Sexually Inappropriate/Disinhibited
　　Behavior
　Wandering/Way-Finding Deficit

Pain Disorder　　　307.xx
　Medical/Medication Issues
　Somatization

**Pain Disorder Associated
with Both Psychological
Factors and a General Medical
Condition**　　　307.89
　Suicidal Ideation/Behavior

**Panic Disorder
with Agoraphobia**　　　300.21
　Anxiety
　Phobia/Panic/Agoraphobia

Somatoform Disorder NOS   300.81
  Somatization

Specific Phobia   300.29
  Anxiety
  Phobia/Panic/Agoraphobia

**Undifferentiated Somatoform
Disorder**   300.81
  Somatization

**Vascular Dementia
with Delusions**   290.42
  Nutritional Deficits Unresolved
  Paranoid Ideation

**Vascular Dementia
with Depressed Mood**   290.43
  Depression
  Spiritual Confusion

BIBLIOGRAPHY

Abeles, N. (ed.). (1997). *What Practitioners Should Know about Working with Older Adults.* Washington, D.C.: American Psychological Association.

American Psychiatric Association. (1994). *Diagnostic and Statistical Manual of Mental Disorders, 4th ed.* Washington, D.C.: American Psychiatric Association.

American Psychiatric Association. (1997). *Practice Guideline for the Treatment of Patients with Alzheimer's Disease and Other Dementias of Late Life.* Washington, D.C.: American Psychiatric Association.

American Psychological Association. (1990). *Guidelines for Providers of Psychological Services to Ethnic, Linguistic, and Culturally Diverse Populations.* Washington, D.C.: American Psychological Association.

Barlow, D. H. (1988). *Anxiety and Its Disorders: The Nature and Treatment of Anxiety and Panic.* New York: Guilford.

Barlow, D. H., and M. G. Craske. (1994). *Mastery of Your Anxiety and Panic (MAP II).* Albany, NY: Graywind Publications.

Camp, C. J., and J. W. Foss. (1997). "Designing Ecologically Valid Memory Interventions for Persons with Dementia." In *Intersections in Basic and Applied Memory Research,* D. G. Payne and F. G. Conrad, eds. Hillsdale, NJ: Erlbaum.

Carstensen, L. L., B. A. Edelstein, and L. Dornbrand (eds.). (1996). *The Practical Handbook of Clinical Gerontology.* Thousand Oaks, CA: Sage.

Cohen, D., and C. Eisdorfer. (1993). *Caring for Your Aging Parents: A Planning and Action Guide.* New York: Putnam.

Costa, P. T., Jr., T. G. Williams, and M. Somerfield. (1996). "Recognition and Initial Assessment of Alzheimer's Disease and Related Dementias." *Clinical Practice Guideline, No. 19.* Rockville, MD: Agency for Health Care Policy and Research, Public Health Service, U.S. Department of Health and Human Services.

Feil, N. (1993). *The Validation Breakthrough: Simple Techniques for Communicating with People with Alzheimer's-Type Dementia.* Baltimore, MD: Health Professions Press.

Folstein, M. F., S. E. Folstein, and P. R. McHugh. (1975). "Mini-mental State: A Practical Method for Grading the Cognitive State of Patients for the Clinician." *Journal of Psychiatric Research, 12,* 189–198.

Gallagher, E., and L. W. Thompson. (1981). *Depression in the Elderly: A Behavioral Treatment Manual.* Los Angeles: The University of Southern California Press.

Hartman-Stein, P. E. (ed.). (1998). *Innovative Behavioral Healthcare for Older Adults: A Guidebook for Changing Times.* San Francisco: Jossey-Bass.

Hussian, R. A., and R. L. Davis. (1985). *Responsive Care: Behavioral Interventions with Elderly Persons.* Champaign, IL: Research Press.

Kane, R. A., and A. L. Caplan (eds.). (1990). *Everyday Ethics: Resolving Dilemmas in Nursing Home Life.* New York: Springer.

Klerman, G. L., S. Budman, D. Berwick, M. M. Weissman, J. Damico-White, A. Demby, and M. Feldstein. (1987). "Efficacy of a Brief Psychosocial Intervention for Symptoms of Stress and Distress among Patients in Primary Care." *Medical Care, 25,* 1078–1088.

Knight, B. G. (1996). *Psychotherapy with Older Adults, 2nd ed.* Boston: Allyn and Bacon.

LaRue, A. (1992). *Aging and Neuropsychological Assessment.* New York: Plenum.

Lawton, M. P., and E. M. Brody. (1969). "Assessment of Older People: Self-Maintaining and Instrumental Activities of Daily Living." *The Gerontologist, 9,* 179–185.

Lichtenberg, P. A. (1994). *A Guide to Psychological Practice in Geriatric Long Term Care.* Binghamton, NY: Haworth Press.

Lichtenberg, P. A., and D. M. Strzepek. (1990). "Assessments of Institutionalized Dementia Patients' Competencies to Participate in Intimate Relationships." *The Gerontologist, 30,* 117–120.

Lichtenberg, P. A., M. Smith, D. Frazer, V. Molinari, E. Rosowsky, R. Crose, N. Stillwell, N. Kramer, P. Hartman-Stein, S. Qualls, M. Salamon, M. Duffy, J. Parr, and D. Gallagher-Thompson. (1998). "Standards for Psychological Services in Long-Term Care Facilities." *The Gerontologist, 38(1),* 122–127.

Mace, N. L., and P. V. Rabins. (1991). *The Thirty-Six-Hour Day: A Family Guide to Caring for Persons with Alzheimer's Disease, Related Dementing Illnesses, and Memory Loss in Later Life.* Baltimore, MD: Johns Hopkins University Press.

McCurry, S. M., R. G. Logsdon, M. V. Vitiello, and L. Teri. (1998). "Successful Behavioral Treatment for Reported Sleep Problems in Elderly Caregivers of Dementia Patients: A Controlled Study." *Journal of Gerontology: Psychological Sciences, 53B,* P122–P129.

Nathan, P. E., and J. M. Gorman (eds.). (1998). *A Guide to Treatments That Work.* New York: Oxford.

National Center for Cost Containment. (1997). *Assessment of Competency and Capacity of the Older Adult: A Practice Guideline for Psychologists.* Washington, D.C.: U.S. Department of Veterans Affairs.

National Center for Cost Containment. (1996). *Geropsychology Assessment Resource Guide.* Washington, D.C.: U.S. Department of Veterans Affairs (PB-96-144365).

Poon, L., T. Crook, K. Davis, C. Eisdorfer, B. Gurland, A. Kaszniak, and L. W. Thompson (eds.). (1989). *Handbook for Clinical Memory Assessment of Older Adults.* Washington, D.C.: American Psychological Association.

Raskin, A., and G. Niederehe (eds.). (1988). "Assessment in Diagnosis and Treatment of Geropsychiatric Patients." *Psychopharmacology Bulletin (Special Feature)*, DHHS Publication No. (ADM) 88-173. Rockville, MD: Department of Health and Human Services, 24(4).

Sheikh, J. I. (1991). "Anxiety Rating Scales for the Elderly." In *Anxiety in the Elderly: Treatment and Research,* C. Salzman and B. D. Lebowitz, eds. New York: Springer Publishing.

Sheikh, J. I., and J. A. Yesavage. (1986). "Geriatric Depression Scale (GDS): Recent Evidence and Development of a Shorter Version." *Clinical Gerontologist, 5,* 165–173.

Stern, L., and J. Fogler. (1988). *Improving Your Memory: A Guide for Older Adults.* Ann Arbor, MI: Memory Skills.

Teri, L. et al. (1994). *Aging and Dementia: Reducing Disability in Alzheimer's Disease. A Manual for Therapists.* Seattle, WA: University of Washington.

Teri, L., and D. Gallagher. (1991). "Cognitive Behavior Interventions for Treatment of Depression." *The Gerontologist, 31,* 413–416.

Teri, L., and Logsdon, R. (1991). Identifying pleasant activities for Alzheimer's disease patients: The Pleasant Events Schedule—AD. *The Gerontologist, 31,* 124–127.

U.S. Department of Health and Human Services, Office of the Inspector General. (1996). *Mental Health Services in Nursing Facilities.* Washington, D.C.: U.S. Department of Health and Human Services.

U.S. Department of Veterans Affairs and University HealthSystem Consortium. (1997). *Dementia Identification and Assessment: Guidelines for Primary Care Practitioners.* Washington, D.C.: U.S. Department of Veterans Affairs.

Wisocki, P. A. (ed.). (1991). *Handbook of Clinical Behavior Therapy with the Elderly Client.* New York: Plenum.

Worden, W. (1991). *Grief Counseling and Grief Therapy, 2nd ed.* New York: Springer.

Yesavage, J. A., T. L. Brink, and T. L. Rose. (1983). "Development and Validation of a Geriatric Depression Scale: A Preliminary Report. *Journal of Psychiatric Residents, 17,* 37–49.

Yesavage, J. A., T. L. Brink, T. Rose, and M. Adey. (1983). "The Geriatric Depression Scale: Comparison with Other Self-Report and Psychiatric Rating Scales. In *Assessment in Geriatric Psychopharmacology,* T. Crook, S. Ferris, and R. Bahrs, eds. New Canaan, CT: Mark Pouley Associates, 152–167.

ABOUT THE DISK*

TheraScribe® 3.0 Library Module Installation

The enclosed disk contains files to upgrade your TheraScribe® 3.0 program to include the behavioral definitions, goals, objectives, interventions, and diagnoses from *The Older Adult Psychotherapy Treatment Planner.*

Note: You must have TheraScribe® 3.0 for Windows installed on your computer to use *The Older Adult Psychotherapy Treatment Planner* library module.

To install the library module, please follow these steps:

1. Place the library module disk in your floppy drive.
2. Log in to TheraScribe® 3.0 as the Administrator using the name "Admin" and your administrator password.
3. On the Main Menu, press the "GoTo" button, and choose the Options menu item.
4. Press the "Import Library" button.
5. On the Import Library Module screen, choose your floppy disk drive a:\ from the list and press "Go." Note: It may take a few minutes to import the data from the floppy disk to your computer's hard disk.
6. When the installation is complete, the library module data will be available in your TheraScribe® 3.0 program.

Note: If you have a network version of TheraScribe® 3.0 installed, you should import the library module one time only. After importing the data, the library module data will be available to all network users.

User Assistance

If you need assistance using this TheraScribe® 3.0 add-on module, contact Wiley Technical Support at:

Phone: 212-850-6753
Fax: 212-850-6800 (Attention: Wiley Technical Support)
Email: techhelp@wiley.com

---

*Note: This section applies only to the book with disk edition, ISBN 0-471-29581-7.

For information on how to install disk, refer to the **About the Disk** section on page 274.

*Note: This section applies only to the book with disk edition, ISBN 0-471-29581-7.

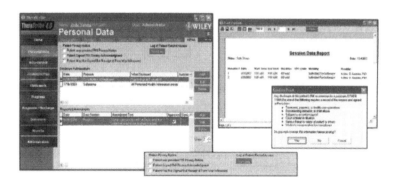

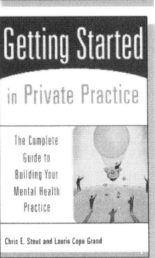

Practice *Planners*

Arthur E. Jongsma, Jr., Series Editor

Helping therapists help their clients...

Treatment Planners cover all the necessary elements for developing formal treatment plans, including detailed problem definitions, long-term goals, short-term objectives, therapeutic interventions, and DSM-IV™ diagnoses.

❑ The Complete Adult Psychotherapy Treatment Planner, Fourth Edition...........0-471-76346-2 / $49.95
❑ The Child Psychotherapy Treatment Planner, Fourth Edition...........................0-471-78535-0 / $49.95
❑ The Adolescent Psychotherapy Treatment Planner, Fourth Edition ....0-471-78539-3 / $49.95
❑ The Addiction Treatment Planner, Third Edition...0-471-72544-7 / $49.95
❑ The Couples Psychotherapy Treatment Planner ....0-471-24711-1 / $49.95
❑ The Group Therapy Treatment Planner, Second Edition...................................0-471-66791-9 / $49.95
❑ The Family Therapy Treatment Planner ....0-471-34768-X / $49.95
❑ The Older Adult Psychotherapy Treatment Planner ....0-471-29574-4 / $49.95
❑ The Employee Assistance (EAP) Treatment Planner ....0-471-24709-X / $49.95
❑ The Gay and Lesbian Psychotherapy Treatment Planner ....0-471-35080-X / $49.95
❑ The Crisis Counseling and Traumatic Events Treatment Planner ....0-471-39587-0 / $49.95
❑ The Social Work and Human Services Treatment Planner ....0-471-37741-4 / $49.95
❑ The Continuum of Care Treatment Planner ....0-471-19568-5 / $49.95
❑ The Behavioral Medicine Treatment Planner...0-471-31923-6 / $49.95
❑ The Mental Retardation and Developmental Disability Treatment Planner ....0-471-38253-1 / $49.95
❑ The Special Education Treatment Planner..0-471-38872-6 / $49.95
❑ The Severe and Persistent Mental Illness Treatment Planner.........................0-471-35945-9 / $49.95
❑ The Personality Disorders Treatment Planner ....0-471-39403-3 / $49.95
❑ The Rehabilitation Psychology Treatment Planner ....0-471-35178-4 / $49.95
❑ The Pastoral Counseling Treatment Planner..0-471-25416-9 / $49.95
❑ The Juvenile Justice and Residential Care Treatment Planner ....0-471-43320-9 / $49.95
❑ The School Counseling and School Social Work Treatment Planner ....0-471-08496-4 / $49.95
❑ The Psychopharmacology Treatment Planner ....0-471-43322-5 / $49.95
❑ The Probation and Parole Treatment Planner...0-471-20244-4 / $49.95
❑ The Suicide and Homicide Risk Assessment
   and Prevention Treatment Planner ....0-471-46631-X / $49.95
❑ The Speech-Language Pathology Treatment Planner..0-471-27504-2 / $49.95
❑ The College Student Counseling Treatment Planner ....0-471-46708-1 / $49.95
❑ The Parenting Skills Treatment Planner ....0-471-48183-1 / $49.95
❑ The Early Childhood Education Intervention Treatment Planner ....0-471-65962-2 / $49.95
❑ The Co-Occurring Disorders Treatment Planner...0-471-73081-5 / $49.95
❑ The Sexual Abuse Victim and Sexual Offender Treatment Planner ....0-471-21979-7 / $49.95
❑ The Complete Women's Psychotherapy Treatment Planner.........................0-470-03983-3 / $49.95

The **Complete Treatment and Homework Planners** series of books combines our bestselling *Treatment Planners* and *Homework Planners* into one easy-to-use, all-in-one resource for mental health professionals treating clients suffering from the most commonly diagnosed disorders.

❑ The Complete Depression Treatment and Homework Planner.....................0-471-64515-X / $39.95
❑ The Complete Anxiety Treatment and Homework Planner ....0-471-64548-6 / $39.95

Over 500,000 Practice *Planners*° sold ...

WILEY

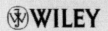

Made in the USA
Lexington, KY
25 November 2010